a biblical guide to

COUNSELING the SEXUALADDICT

STEVE GALLAGHER

Also Available by Steve Gallagher:
Out of the Depths of Sexual Sin
At the Altar of Sexual Idolatry
At the Altar of Sexual Idolatry Workbook
Living in Victory
Break Free from the Lusts of This World
The Walk of Repentance
Irresistible to God

For these books and other teaching materials contact:
Pure Life Ministries
14 School St.
Dry Ridge, KY 41035
(888)293-8714 - toll-free order line
(859)824-4444 - office
(859)813-0005 - FAX
www.purelifeministries.org
inquire@purelifeministries.org

A Bibilical Guide to Counseling the Sexual Addict
Copyright © 2004 by Steve Gallagher
All rights reserved. No part of this book may be reproduced
in any form except for brief quotations, without
written permission from the author.

ISBN 0-9715470-9-2

Note: This book has been written as a complement to
At the Altar of Sexual Idolatry. It is assumed that the reader is already familiar
with its concepts.

ACKNOWLEDGEMENTS

My special thanks to Scott Cochran and Bradley Furges for all of their valuable contributions to the writing of this book.

DEDICATION

I dedicate this book to the countless pastors, counselors
and lay leaders who have committed themselves to
providing biblical solutions, godly leadership and sacrificial
service to those who struggle with habitual sexual sin.

TABLE OF CONTENTS

FOREWORD

When I first met Steve Gallagher at a Biblical counseling conference I sensed I had met a partner in the battle for truth. I had watched TV interviews of self-proclaimed experts on "sexual addictions" promote standard psychological dogma in the name of Christ. I had heard well-known Christian psychologists tell their radio listeners that obsession with pornography, perversion and adultery are results of unmet needs and childhood traumas. So when I heard of Pure Life Ministries, I wondered if they too would provide the same old excuses for immorality and offer one more failing variation of Christian psychotherapy to treat this growing scourge.

Steve and I talked for quite some time about the weakening of the Church by well-meaning, but misguided counselors who believe that the Bible is insufficient to heal the wounded hearts of damaged Christians. I was encouraged to hear Steve's heart-felt commitment to genuine Biblical counseling and its application to sexual idolatry.

Pure Life Ministries eventually applied for affiliate membership with the International Association of Biblical Counselors and our vice president went on site at their Kentucky campus to examine their doctrines and practice. To our delight, he found an organization that takes the Scriptures seriously and is committed to helping fallen Christians find their way back to a strong walk with the Lord.

That's why I am pleased to recommend *A Biblical Guide to Counseling the Sexual Addict*. In this book Steve Gallagher lays out a powerful model for counseling "sexual addicts" in a Biblical manner. He does not use the term "addiction" to indicate a disease or to lessen personal responsibility for one's behavior; rather, it is shorthand for life-dominating sexual sins that can be conquered through the Word of God and intense discipleship.

Steve writes with the authority of one who has experienced the pain and devastation of the downward spiral of sexual idolatry, and his subsequent victory and restoration through the powerful work of the Holy Spirit as he submitted to the Scriptures. This is not a book of theory, but of proven successful practice taking place continually at the Pure Life Ministries campus.

The Pure Life Live-In Program requires at least a six-month commitment where counselees are taught Scriptural principles of Christian lifestyle through ongoing instruction, Biblical homework, regular chores, intensive prayer, in-depth Bible study, supportive fellowship and one-on-one counseling. Worship services are held three times a week in the PLM chapel in order to help the men develop a spiritual hunger to know and please God. Through this powerful regimen, many have been set free and have seen their broken marriages restored.

But Pure Life Ministries is limited in how many applicants they can accept, due to the constraints of their facilities and finances. That's the reason for a book such as this – to provide a practical Biblical model for churches and counselors who wish to replicate this sort of ministry in their own communities.

In the first section of this volume, Steve explains the fundamentals of Biblical counseling as they relate to sexual sin. Then he shares specific applications of the principles when dealing with the temptations facing young people, helping the devastated wife who discovers her husband's infidelity, ministering to the homosexual, and when confronting the pastor who struggles with pornography and other sexual sins. In the final section, Steve explains how to begin a ministry of support for those who have fallen into sexual idolatry. Imagine a Pure Life Ministry campus in every State where people can be set free!

We in the International Association of Biblical Counselors are thankful to partner with people like Steve and Kathy Gallagher and the committed Staff of Pure Life Ministries. May our Lord help us all to return to the Word of God to find lasting healing for sin-damaged lives and devastated marriages.

Dr. Ed Bulkley, President
International Association of
Biblical Counselors

INTRODUCTION

When I entered the ministry in 1986, I could have never guessed that my life's calling would be to minister to men in habitual sexual sin. Sexual addiction was a concept almost unheard of in those days. All these years later, I can honestly say that it has been my privilege to devote my life to helping these men.

Having since encountered thousands of men bound up in sexual sin, I have gotten a fairly good sense about what the typical sexual addict is like. The first place to begin one's preparation for providing help is to understand what the man in habitual sexual sin* is like. In that light, I will attempt to draw a composite picture of him.

The typical man who will come to you for help has been involved in illicit sexual activity for years. This immoral lifestyle has been done almost entirely in secret. Although sexual fantasy, pornography and illicit encounters make up a huge part of his life, he has managed to hide it from most, if not all, of his closest friends and

---

*I use the term man loosely, and again, for the sake of simplicity. There are more female sexual addicts today than ever before.

relatives. Most acquaintances would consider him to be morally upright and would never guess what he does when no one is looking.

At different times, you will undoubtedly find yourself helping men who frequent adult bookstores, strip clubs, massage parlors and prostitutes. You may also be forced to minister to men involved with peeking in windows, exposing themselves to women, making obscene telephone calls, sexually assaulting others, or even having sex with animals. You will most certainly deal with promiscuity among teenagers and adults. You will also probably minister to homosexuals—both male and female. However, the primary recipients of your attention will be men who are simply addicted to pornography.

At any rate, the average man you will encounter in your work has been faithfully attending church services for many years. He also reads inspirational books, listens to Christian radio, and possibly attends special men's events.

Unfortunately, the fact that he has been involved in so much religious activity has very possibly hurt him more than it has helped. Sitting in church on Sunday and viewing the filthy images of pornography during the week only tends to harden a man's heart and deepen his spiritual delusion. Sin always deceives. The more wickedness a person is involved in, the blinder he will become to his true spiritual condition. Because he senses God's presence in meetings, it is easy for him to imagine that he truly is walking closely with the Lord. This is compounded by the spiritual reality that the Lord is not quick to judge sin.

This double life of outward Christianity and hidden sin distorts reality and brings confusion. In my book, *At the Altar of Sexual Idolatry*, I wrote the following about this phenomenon:

Darkness of mind signifies the lack of light in a person's thinking. The more a person gives himself over to the power of sin, the harder he grows toward God. He may still attend church, sing all of the songs of worship, and even enjoy good preaching, but there is a thick callous around his heart that keeps him from feeling the Holy Spirit nudge him toward repentance. The more a person sins, the thicker that callous grows. Eventually he will find himself so hardened that he can no longer discern truth for himself. Although he is likely to still have some comprehension for doctrinal truth, *the* Truth has been effectively shut out of his heart.[1]

Living in spiritual defeat over a prolonged period of time causes the man to waffle back and forth between an inflated sense of his own spirituality and a feeling of overwhelming hopelessness. Part of the problem is that for years he has run to books, seminars and support group meetings in the hopes that he can overcome his problems with a minimal amount of effort. His dilemma has been exacerbated because he has gotten his hopes up many times over the years by the exaggerated claims of people offering help: "Read this book, it's powerful!" "This seminar will change your life!" He dutifully reads those books and attends those seminars but finds that nothing has changed. Each promising situation that doesn't bring victory leaves him more cynical. After a while, he even becomes skeptical about the promises held out by Scripture.

This is the man who will one day come to you for answers. If you are going to offer him real help, you will have to understand the realm in which he lives.

Ministering in a Sexualized Culture

Men involved in pornography and sexual sin are simply by-products of the world in which they live. An immoral mindset has gripped America—indeed, the entire Western Civilization. We have slipped far away from the decency that once established acceptable standards for our nation. That morality is now openly scoffed as prudish and old-fashioned. Lewd conduct is now the norm: a president having illicit encounters with a young intern in the Oval Office, homosexuality flagrantly displayed on TV sitcoms, a famous entertainer being mobbed by his adoring fans hours after being indicted for child molestation, two female pop stars kissing on national television, etc. These incidents, and thousands like them, occur everyday in modern America.

According to researchers, pornography is now a $10 billion annual industry—larger than the annual revenues from major league baseball, the NFL and the NBA combined! That constitutes an 1,800% increase in the past five years.[2] There are over two million websites with adult content[3] and approximately "25 million Americans visit cyber-sex sites between 1-10 hours per week. Another 4.7 million in excess of 11 hours per week."[4]

Over the years, a number of disturbing facts have emerged about the effects pornography has on its viewers. Obscene material promotes:

- Sexual addiction and promiscuity.
- Unhealthy attitudes about sexuality.
- The dehumanization of women as sex toys.
- The rape myth, that women actually want to be raped.
- Sexual relationships apart from love and commitment.

- Selfish indulgence and isolation.
- Aberrant and bizarre sex.

The Church has not been immune from this moral disaster either. Surprisingly enough, studies and polls have shown that the percentage of Christian men regularly viewing pornography is the same as that of nonbelievers (about 20%). According to a poll conducted by Christianity Today in 2001, 44% of pastors acknowledged that they had visited a smut site.[5] There is every reason to believe that these percentages have grown substantially since then.

A GREAT NEED

The need has never been greater for godly men and women to reach out to these struggling individuals and their devastated families. Indeed, many are doing so. However, there is a direct correlation between a counselor's* methods and the effectiveness of his efforts in helping these hurting people.

If you are increasingly confronted with those in sexual sin, I encourage you to become thoroughly prepared and then confidently enter the battle, fully assured that God will bless your efforts. You will embark on a thrilling journey that will certainly bring forth abundant fruit. Jesus Christ was called "a friend of sinners." This is a badge of honor in the Kingdom of God that you will wear as well. Nothing could possibly be more pleasing to God than for a Christian to lay down his life on behalf of those devastated by sin.

---

*This book is written to pastors, ministers, counselors and lay leaders. However, for the sake of simplicity, I will simply use the term counselor throughout the book.

BOOK ONE

APPLYING THE FUNDAMENTALS
OF BIBLICAL COUNSELING

Do not be surprised, brethren, if the world hates you. We know that we have passed out of death into life, because we love the brethren. He who does not love abides in death. Everyone who hates his brother is a murderer; and you know that no murderer has eternal life abiding in him.

We know love by this, that He laid down His life for us; and we ought to lay down our lives for the brethren. But whoever has the world's goods, and sees his brother in need and closes his heart against him, how does the love of God abide in him? Little children, let us not love with word or with tongue, but in deed and truth. (I John 3:13-18)

THE FOUNDATION OF OUR COUNSEL

Brethren, if any person is overtaken in any conduct or sin of any sort, you who are spiritual, who are responsive to and controlled by the Spirit, should set him right and restore and reinstate him, without any sense of superiority and with all gentleness keeping an attentive eye on yourself lest you should be tempted also. Bear, endure, carry, one another's burdens and troublesome moral faults and in this way fulfill and observe perfectly the law of Christ. (Galatians 6:1-2 AMP)

As a result of the Sexual Revolution, millions of men (and women) are in terrible bondage to sexual sin. There exists a great need for qualified Christians to step into this spiritual cesspool and help these troubled souls find freedom. I am certain that the Lord is calling His people to meet this need. However, those who sense that call must properly prepare themselves for the inevitable battle.

In the Scripture passage above, Paul outlines the requirements of a person wishing to help those who have fallen into sin. We will examine his three imperatives in this chapter.

THOSE WHO ARE SPIRITUAL

Paul's opening remarks clearly indicate those who should be involved in this work: "you who are spiritual, who are responsive to and controlled by the Spirit." He establishes the context for this conditional statement in the preceding chapter where he summarizes spirituality in three basic characteristics:

1. A believer who has a history of crucifying "the flesh and its passions and desires," (vs. 17, 24);
2. A believer who is led, controlled and influenced by the Holy Spirit (vs. 16, 18, 25);
3. A believer whose life manifests the fruit of the Spirit (vs. 21-22).

Since his remarks establish the qualifications for those ministering to habitual sinners, these traits warrant at least a brief examination.

Galatians 5:16-17 describes the conflict between the Spirit and flesh that rages within every believer. The "flesh" is a term Paul uses to describe man's lower nature: that part of every human that selfishly desires pleasure, prominence, comfort, entertainment, and so on. The saints he refers to as "spiritual" have reached their level of maturity by waging a life-long war with the appetites of the flesh. Although they lost many of these skirmishes in their early years, what stands out about them is that they refused to quit fighting until their passions had been crucified and brought under subjection to the Holy Spirit. They are deemed "spiritual" because their daily lives are much more taken up with their life in God than in "the desires of the flesh."

To "walk by" or be "led by" the Spirit means that a person's thinking has come under God's control through this process of crucifixion. To be able to help others in spiritual turmoil one must first undergo the process of brokenness in one's own life. I expounded on this phenomenon in another book:

> In First Corinthians One, Paul describes what we would call "the Western Mind." He says, "The Greeks [Gentiles] seek after wisdom." (I Corinthians 1:22) This proclivity to exalt human wisdom is a primary roadblock facing believers who want deep, true, victorious living in Christ Jesus. God doesn't expect us to be mindless morons, but He does command us to "set our minds on things above" and seek the mind of Christ in all things. Our problem stems from our tendency to approach spiritual matters with the natural, reasoning mind, which is a perpetual antagonist of God. Paul said that "the mind set on the flesh is hostile toward God; for it does not subject itself to the law of God, for it is not even able to do so." (Romans 8:7) His point is that the natural processes of the human mind work completely differently than those of the Spirit. Humans are inherently self-centered; our thinking constantly revolves around self. The pride and selfishness that result from this kind of thinking are in opposition to the way the Spirit of God thinks. Because a basic conflict exists between the two (Galatians 5:17), even the most brilliant person will unfortunately never enter the Kingdom of God unless he humbles himself as a little child. Jesus said, "Truly I say to you, unless you are converted and become like children, you shall not enter the kingdom of heaven. Whoever then humbles himself as this child, he is the greatest in the kingdom of

heaven." (Matthew 18:3-4) As believers it is imperative that we come down out of our high-mindedness and learn that spiritual problems cannot be understood or deduced through the logical reasoning of the human mind.[1]

Lastly, the "spiritual" manifest the fruit of the Spirit in their daily lives. Love—whole-hearted devotion to God—is the life force that permeates the being of those who are full of the Holy Spirit. The secret of their indescribable joy lies in the fact that their hearts are perpetually turned toward the One they love. Nothing can disturb the peace—the tranquility of soul—of the saint who constantly communes with God. Out of this rich life in God comes the loveliness of character described in the following terms: patience, kindness, goodness, faithfulness, gentleness, self-control.

With all of this in mind, let us briefly review what some commentators say about those whom Paul calls "spiritual." Robertson's Word Pictures in the New Testament concisely defined this term as, "The spiritually led (Gal 5:18), the spiritual experts in mending souls."[2] Dr. John Gill described them as those "such as live and walk in the Spirit, and are strong, and stand by the power and grace of the Spirit of God…"[3] Adam Clarke said that they "have wisdom and experience in Divine things…"[4] Albert Barnes wrote that they are those "Who are under the influences of the Holy Spirit… holy persons…"[5] Finally, Dr. George Findlay remarked that they have "a knowledge of the human heart, a self-restraint and patient skill…"[6]

The inescapable fact is that mere dissemination of facts on sexual addiction will not touch a heart that is hardened by years of sin. Frankly, if the counselor is not walking in the Spirit, he will not be much help to the man coming to him in deep need. Indeed, he will discover that a Christian leader can only take someone to the same depths he himself has gone. Only God has the power to transform a person's heart and only the godly have the spiritual expertise to offer any real help.

In the introduction, we discussed the great depravity of the sexual addict. Men in this spiritual condition need a counselor who is connected to God. Book knowledge about the problem has its place, but that alone is not sufficient to help another. The man actively indulging in the "deeds of the flesh" desperately needs help from someone whose life is exhibiting "the fruit of the Spirit." He needs personal ministry from someone who is feasting daily on the riches of God. "The teaching of the wise is a fountain of life, to turn aside from the snares of death." (Proverbs 13:14)

THE RESTORATION PROCESS

Having established the qualifications for helping those in habitual sin, Paul next explains the process of restoration. The word "restore" used here (Gk. katartizo) is the same word used by physicians to describe the setting of a broken bone. What an apt picture of the man who has been involved in pornography and/or fornication! He may seemingly have it all together—holding down a responsible position, taking care of his family, going to church. He outwardly personifies the all-American life. However, inwardly he has been crushed to pieces by the destructive nature of sin. His perspectives on sexuality are warped and distorted. Evil darkness has penetrated his heart and clouded his thinking. Spiritually speaking, he has fallen off a three story building: he's still alive, but he's all busted up inside. He needs someone who can help him set things in order.*

The counselor's primary role in the restoration process is to lead the counselee into a biblical mindset using correction from God's Word. Although an essential key in helping men overcome habitual sin, confronting people in the right spirit is one of the most difficult things a counselor will ever do. Biblical confrontation requires the perfect balance of grace and truth personified by Jesus. Any study of His dealings with others clearly reveals that He was an absolute expert at meeting people's deepest spiritual needs. He could do this because He was "full of grace and truth." (John 1:14)

Bringing correction into a person's life is a delicate operation requiring great care. No one would even consider operating on a person's spinal cord, and yet it is amazing how some will recklessly delve into another's fragile inner world with little expertise!** The counsel of the unqualified discipler usually strays off course either by overemphasizing grace at the expense of truth or vice-versa. The results are potentially disastrous!

A person attempting to break free from habitual sin needs encouragement. However, if that is all he receives from his counselor there will be minimal change in his life. It is good

---

* Paul encountered people in his day that also had an exaggerated opinion of their fitness to minister: "But the goal of instruction is love from a pure heart and a good conscience and a sincere faith. For some men, straying from these things, have turned aside to fruitless discussions, wanting to be teachers of the Law, even though they do not understand either what they are saying or the matters about which they make confident assertions." (1 Timothy 1:5-7)

** I should take a moment here to establish a spiritual fact that is important to understand: every human being alive is "out of whack" in many ways spiritually. No matter how emotionally together a person appears, God sees a different picture. His great desire is to mold humans into the image of His Son. This is the process of sanctification.

to feel sympathy and even pity for those who are struggling. However, human mercy, in itself, always tends to see a person's need in temporal rather than eternal terms.

One example of this occurred while Jesus was sharing with His disciples how the religious leaders of Israel would put Him to death. Peter, in his unbroken condition, could not accept this. Indignant and full of humanistic mercy, he took Jesus aside and rebuked Him. Picture it—a man rebuking God! And yet, what a perfect example of someone thinking he can discern needs better than the Lord. Imagine Peter's shock when Jesus turned to him and said, "Get behind Me, Satan! You are a stumbling block to Me; for you are not setting your mind on God's interests, but man's." Jesus then said to His disciples, "If anyone wishes to come after Me, let him deny himself, and take up his cross, and follow Me. For whoever wishes to save his life shall lose it; but whoever loses his life for My sake shall find it. For what will a man be profited, if he gains the whole world, and forfeits his soul? Or what will a man give in exchange for his soul?" (Matthew 16:23-26) The clear implication here is that Peter's human pity for Jesus was built upon the sandy soil of temporal ease. Saving one's life in this world is actually Satan's perversion of mercy. However, a person who is not walking in the Spirit can interpret it as kindness while interpreting God's mercy as cruelty!

In the existing field of counseling, this secularized mercy usually takes the form of therapies that focus on feelings rather than spirituality. There is, of course, nothing inherently wrong in feeling sympathy for a person's emotional pain. Indeed, when a Christian becomes involved in the struggles of others, he will undoubtedly encounter some heartbreaking stories. However, he cannot allow pity to supersede God's Word in establishing a course of action for counseling that person.

The greatest mercy a counselor can do for the man living in rebellion against God's law is to help him discover genuine repentance and restoration. Biblical reproof, then, becomes essential in enabling the man to see authentic repentance as his avenue to freedom.

The man entrenched in a pattern of licentiousness needs someone who will stand against his flesh during those times of spiritual weakness. When he strays off course, the ultimate kindness one can do is to stop him from foolishly plunging into the abyss. However, I can attest (after many years of experience) that there's nothing quite so difficult as confronting someone in the right spirit. It requires a great deal of selfless love. It's costly, but anything less is not of God.

In addition to offering encouragement, a counselor must also lovingly speak the truth. Unfortunately, some fall prey to the selfish enjoyment of pointing out others' faults. Pride, rather than love, compels them and gives them a feeling of superiority.

The counselor, who is not in a spirit of meekness, will become critical, self-righteous and hardhearted toward people's needs. As a Christian learns to counsel biblically, he will become more adept at spiritual discernment. In the right spirit, he will perceive sin in the lives of others but through eyes of love. However, if he himself is unbroken and unconquered by God, he will see the same problems, only with a critical spirit.

A number of years ago, Kathy and I developed a relationship with the pastor of the church we were attending. He seemed quite interested in helping us personally, so we humbled ourselves to receive whatever spiritual guidance he could give. Kathy and I held the conviction that, since we were in the business of bringing correction to others, we should always be willingly vulnerable to other ministers.

During their first counseling appointment, Kathy really opened herself up to this pastor. Unbeknownst to us, he had recently grown frustrated with us over some petty issues in the church and took full advantage of this opportunity to confront her about issues in her life that he felt were un-Christlike. While a portion of his criticism was legitimate, much of it was unfounded, and the entire spirit in the delivery was wrong. Kathy, having been schooled in humility, did absolutely nothing to defend herself. Finally, after three emotionally grueling hours, she left his office—devastated.

The upside to this story is that it sensitized us both to how easy it is to hurt others when confronting sin. The reality is that an acute awareness of people's faults can be dangerous. The spirit a counselor is in will determine his ability to act accordingly. Paul, conveying this same truth, says that the minister "should set him right and restore and reinstate him, without any sense of superiority and with all gentleness keeping an attentive eye on yourself lest you should be tempted also." (Galatians 6:1)

Elsewhere in Scripture, Paul states it this way: "And the Lord's bond-servant must not be quarrelsome, but be kind to all, able to teach, patient when wronged, with gentleness correcting those who are in opposition, if perhaps God may grant them repentance leading to the knowledge of the truth, and they may come to their senses and escape from the snare of the devil, having been held captive by him to do his will." (II Timothy 2:24-26)

Bringing godly correction into another's life is difficult, but if done in the right spirit, it could potentially save him from destruction. If a man knows that you love him, he will accept your reproof. In fact, if he knows that you are doing it out of sincere concern for his well being, he will often be grateful.* Matthew Henry said, "He has done about half his work in convincing another of error who has first convinced him that he loves him."[7]

The key to biblical confrontation is maintaining the proper balance between grace and truth. My personal testimony is this: if you will allow the Holy Spirit to direct your counsel, many men will respond and the results will be astounding!

BEARING THE SINNER

In his instructions about helping the habitual sinner, Paul also admonishes the spiritual leader to, "Bear, endure, carry, one another's burdens and troublesome moral faults and in this way fulfill and observe perfectly the law of Christ." What, you may ask, is the "law of Christ" that Paul refers to here? He identifies it in the previous chapter: "For the whole Law is fulfilled in one word, in the statement, 'You shall love your neighbor as yourself.'"

Paul's meaning is unmistakable: To help people overcome habitual sin, you must consider their needs as important as your own. In meeting people's needs, you manifest the practical love of a passionate God. The habitual sinner needs a godly person who bears him to God in this way. I can't state this strongly enough: Please be prepared to bear people spiritually before becoming deeply involved in their lives. They desperately need care from someone with the desire and capability to spiritually carry them.

---

* It should be noted that this isn't always the case. Many men do not want the truth and will resent the person who brings it. Solomon rightly said, "He who corrects a scoffer gets dishonor for himself, and he who reproves a wicked man gets insults for himself. Do not reprove a scoffer, lest he hate you, reprove a wise man, and he will love you." (Proverbs 9:7-8) However, when you love a person, you often have to bring the reproof in spite of the fact that he might lash out at you in anger.

In his epistle to the Romans, Paul states it in a slightly different manner: "Now we who are strong ought to bear the weaknesses of those without strength and not just please ourselves. Let each of us please his neighbor for his good, to his edification. For even Christ did not please Himself..." (Romans 15:1-3)

Bearing people in this way requires deep involvement in their lives. Paul, again addressing the Roman church, provides the complete picture:

Be devoted to one another in brotherly love; give preference to one another in honor; not lagging behind in diligence, fervent in spirit, serving the Lord; rejoicing in hope, persevering in tribulation, devoted to prayer, contributing to the needs of the saints, practicing hospitality. Bless those who persecute you; bless and curse not. Rejoice with those who rejoice, and weep with those who weep. Be of the same mind toward one another; do not be haughty in mind, but associate with the lowly. Do not be wise in your own estimation. Never pay back evil for evil to anyone. Respect what is right in the sight of all men. (Romans 12:10-17)

What stands out in this passage is the extreme sacrifice required of Christians who devote themselves to helping others. The counselor who bears the sexual sinner must walk into the cesspool of his life and help drag him out. I can say from experience—it's impossible to remain clean while wading into such a mess. It also means making yourself available to them at all times, day or night.

Finally, bearing a person spiritually requires intercession. For the shackles of sin to be broken in a man's life, someone has to bear him before the throne of grace. Consistent, fervent prayer allows God to come in and do a work in a struggling person's life. As I've already stated, only God can transform the human heart.

Let us now reconsider the appalling spiritual condition of the habitual sexual sinner: His hardened heart is shrouded in deep darkness. The insanity of pride and delusion has created a spiritual blindness. His terrible condition will not be rectified by giving him a few spiritual pointers. The Holy Spirit alone has the power to bring order out of such chaos. Human advice, in itself, is not the answer. The counselor's prayers are the catalyst by which God goes to work on the man's behalf. Effectual, fervent prayers change lives.

The Lord taught me an important lesson about this one bitterly cold Chicago morning in 1992 while on one of my customary prayer walks. As I trudged through a deserted park at 5 a.m., the Lord gave me a mental picture of His work through Pure Life Ministries. In my mind's eye, I saw myself holding a long plank over my shoulders. On it were all of my staff members, only seven at that time, each of them holding a plank of his own. On their planks were their counselees. I sensed the Lord calling me to make intercession on behalf of my workers one of my primary duties in ministry. As I continually held them up to God in prayer, asking Him to supply them with the strength and grace to do their jobs, they, in turn, were to intercede for each of their counselees. For the most part, the PLM staff has been faithful to this charge. Thus, it is now required of every worker at Pure Life to spend at least two hours each morning with the Lord. This is a very real picture of what it means to bear people to God. Men's lives are being radically transformed in our residential facility, not due to some great counseling system, but because there are people really praying for them.

Ministering to those ravaged by the effects of sexual sin is never glamorous. It is a dirty business, to be sure. Often, as I travel around the country speaking in different ministry settings, I encounter others teaching on the subject of sexual sin. It is remarkable how few of them truly know what it means to bear someone spiritually. At various conferences, they present their own personally-developed ideas, but most have little experience in the day-to-day, hands-on involvement. The true counseling warrior makes necessary spiritual sacrifices to stand against others' flesh and bear them to God.

THE CRUX OF OUR COUNSEL

E mbedded within every man's soul are two intensely related passions that demand fulfillment—sexuality and
spirituality. God created sex to be a source of pleasure
as well as a deeply spiritual expression of marital love. Thus, a
believer's relationship with God is often equated with that between husband and wife. (cf. Hosea 1-2; Revelation 21)

Unfortunately, some Christian men recklessly allow their
carnal desires to run amok. Rather than seeking oneness with
God through worship and with their wives through sexual
intimacy, they cross over into sexual perversion. At this point,
reason is abandoned and perspectives are skewed. Contrary
to God's original design, man's dual passions then become
fused into a distorted, irresistible drive to worship *at the altar
of sexual idolatry.*

Men who undertake this plunge into corruption find it a
daunting task to regain the innocence they willfully relin-
quished. Even more difficult is the restoration of fractured
relationships with God, their wives and others. Regardless
of the dire consequences of sin, however, there is a way of
escape! Counselors must help these men to see that freedom

is available but only through deep repentance, a renewed, godly perspective on sexuality, and an understanding of true worship.

Understanding The Full Scope Of Worship

In both the Hebrew and Greek lexicons, the term *worship* conveys the idea of physically prostrating oneself before another. In fact, the Greek term takes it even further, giving the sense of a person bowing down in utmost humility to kiss the hand of someone superior.

Humans are, by design, worshippers. They are constantly prostrating themselves in their hearts to something or someone. Situated in the soul of every man is a spiritual altar, and seated on that altar is *the* most important object of his life. Whether he realizes it or not, the concept of worship involves far more than singing a few hymns and choruses on Sunday mornings. Worship is a not just an act or occasion; it is a lifestyle in which one pays homage to the supreme object of his desire.

When a person allows something other than God to take preeminence in his life, the object of adoration becomes an idol. It displaces the Lord's rightful position of worship in the heart. For most people, idols arise from those things or experiences the spirit of this world offers, which cater to "the lust of the flesh, and the lust of the eyes, and the pride of life..." and thereby dictate the course of their lives. However, as any diligent student of the Bible knows, the first commandment makes it clear that God will not tolerate this: "You shall have no other gods before Me... You shall not worship them or serve them; for I, the LORD your God, am a jealous God..." (Exodus 20:3-5)

Jesus said it this way: "Where your treasure is, there will your heart be also." The willful decision to turn your heart away from the Lord in favor of an idol is an abomination to God. Because of the powerful nature of worship, it is extremely dangerous to worship the created thing rather than the Creator.

Not only does idolatry seduce a person away from the Lord, it also molds the idolater into the image of his chosen desire. (Psalm 115:8) In other words, a person becomes like the thing he cherishes most. Rather than being "conformed to the image of His Son," (Romans 8:29) he is being "conformed to the pattern of this world." (Romans 12:2 NIV) Thus, the man who actively worships *at the altar of sexual idolatry* will increasingly exhibit the demonic characteristics of the object of his adoration.

This truth is powerfully displayed in the recent movie trilogy, *Lord of the Rings*, based on the books by J.R.R. Tolkein. Throughout the story, Smeagol's obsession with the Ring of Power gradually turns him into the beastly creature Gollum. Scripture could have been describing him when it stated, "Let the evil-doer do worse and worse, let the base grow baser and baser, let the upright man be more and more upright, and the man who is holy be more and more holy." (Revelation 22:11, Goodspeed) A.W. Tozer brings this out brilliantly:

> We are all in process of becoming. We have already moved from what we were to what we are, and we are now moving toward what we shall be…
>
> The perturbing thought is not that we are becoming, but what we are becoming; not that we are moving, but toward what we are moving. For it is not in human nature to move on a horizontal plane; we are either ascending or descending, mounting up or sinking down. When a moral being travels from

one to another position, it must always be toward the worse or toward the better...

It has been established here, I hope, that human nature is in a formative state and that it is being changed into the image of the thing it loves. Men and women are being molded by their affinities, shaped by their affections and powerfully transformed by the artistry of their loves. In the unregenerate world of Adam this produces day-by-day tragedies of cosmic proportions. Think of the power that turned an innocent pink-cheeked boy into a Nero or a Himmler. And was Jezebel always the "cursed woman" whose head and hands the very dogs, with poetic justice, refused to eat? No; once she dreamed her pure girlish dreams and blushed at the thoughts of womanly love; but soon she became interested in evil things, admired them and went on at last to love them. There the law of moral affinity took over and Jezebel, like clay in the hand of the potter, was turned to the deformed and hateful thing that the chamberlains threw down from the window.[1]

THE LOVE OF PLEASURE

God created a world full of simple, unadulterated pleasures for His creatures to enjoy. However, untold multitudes—including many churchgoers—refuse God's original design and make pleasure the god of their life. They are known as *hedonists*. When pleasure of any sort—even sexual pleasure—becomes the focal point of one's daily existence, it not only eats away at a person's spiritual life, but it eventually contaminates everything that is wholesome.

Jesus said that the love of pleasure chokes out the Word

of God. (Luke 8:14) James told his constituents that their love for pleasure thwarted their prayers and kept them in a spirit of lust. (James 4:1-3) The writer of Hebrews held Moses up as an example to us all because he chose "rather to endure ill-treatment with the people of God, than to enjoy the passing pleasures of sin." (Hebrews 11:25) And, the apostle Paul spoke of those who are "enslaved to various lusts and pleasures." (Titus 3:3)

While these passages are each uniquely profound, it is Paul's prophetic words in II Timothy 3:4-5 that are most alarming. There the apostle speaks of those living in the last days who are "lovers of pleasure rather than lovers of God; holding to a form of godliness, although they have denied its power..." Undoubtedly, this passage of Scripture refers to people who make pleasure their *raison d'etre*—their supreme purpose in life. Though exhibiting "a form of godliness," the true object of their undying affections is not God but pleasure itself.

The person who has sexual pleasure as his focus of worship—whether or not he considers himself to be a Christian—will find that he increasingly resembles that idol.

TRUE REPENTANCE:
PRECURSOR TO REAL CHANGE

No minister of the gospel should need convincing that illicit sexual behavior is sinful. However, over the last 20-30 years, a great transformation of thought has swept the Church into complacency. Under the guise of progressiveness, the Holy Ghost-inspired cry for holiness that used to thunder from pulpits has, to a large extent, been supplanted by "scientific" rationalizations for man's behavior. Instead of being encouraged to seek godly repentance with tears of contrition at the foot of Calvary, the lust-filled, sex-crazed man is given license to justify and excuse his sin and thereby avoid taking proper responsibility for his own actions.* This silencing of the Holy Spirit's conviction is unspeakably tragic given that repentance is God's *only* solution to habitual sin.

The sad reality is that most Christian men involved in habitual sexual sin have spent years riding the merry-go-round of sin and false repentance, never finding the breakthrough into freedom they seem so desperately to seek. Elsewhere I explained it this way:

As the (sexual) addict enters the beginning stage of remorse, he will often make certain promises to God vowing never to repeat the same sin again: "Lord, I swear I won't do this ever again!" As his eyes are opened to the reality of the horrible emptiness and nature of his sin, he readily makes such a vow; for, it is at this moment that he truly sees sin for what it really is.

However, the problem with making such a resolution is that it stems from the man's own strength and determination to resist and overcome an evil. This sort of "promise-keeping" will never endure future temptations in the same area. It is for this exact reason that the sex addict has attempted countless times before to break the habit, yet to no avail.

The man desperately needs repentance. True

---

* After speaking to a group of ministers recently on the subject of ministering to homosexuals, a young homosexual "Christian" approached me and, without batting an eye, told me that he had never had homosexual lust; he had been involved in the "lifestyle" because he had emotional needs that had not been met as a child. Hence, he had nothing to feel remorseful about and did not sense any need to repent.

repentance comes when a man's heart has changed its outlook on sin. A man will only quit his sinful, destructive behavior when he has truly repented of it in his heart.[2]

To grasp true repentance, one must comprehend the nature of sin. A person sins whenever he willfully acts upon a fleshly impulse to do something that has been forbidden by God. In other words, he rejects God's will in favor of his own. So, any attempt to find freedom from habitual sin while remaining in self-will is futile. The act of repentance involves a confession that one's behavior is wrong, a commitment to quit that behavior, and a submission to God's will. "Godly sorrow" that "produces a repentance without regret" (cf. II Corinthians 7:10) occurs when the person realizes the error of his ways and agrees to change.

In the pivotal Chapter 13 of *At the Altar of Sexual Idolatry*, I broke the process down into four basic components:

1. Poverty of spirit: seeing one's need to change and coming to the realization that he cannot accomplish this change without the power of God.
2. Mourning over sin: as the person begins to face the ugliness of his behavior, he becomes broken over it.
3. Submission to God: as the sin in one's heart is exposed, true repentance occurs. Self-will is replaced by submission to God's authority.
4. Fruits of repentance: as God is allowed to conquer the man's heart, a change occurs which becomes evident in the way he lives his life.

It is vital that you, as counselor, lead the man out of

habitual sin and into this kind of genuine repentance. He cannot conjure up this experience for himself. He must seek God for it. The counselor's role is helping the counselee see his need for a radical inward transformation and praying that he receives it.*

THE PLACE OF WORSHIP

While it is absolutely imperative that the struggling sinner experience true repentance, that is only part of the process of change. Yes, he must turn *away* from sin, but he must also turn *toward* God. He must stop worshipping the idol of sex and begin truly worshipping God.** This is the most significant crossroads the man will ever face.

However, a counselor telling him that he needs to learn how to worship God may only confuse or even anger him. After all, this is a man who has been singing songs of "worship" in church for years. Unfortunately, in his utter delusion, he fails to realize his "worship" has contained very little spiritual reality. In essence, he has been living in open defiance against the Lord. However, if he enters into authentic repentance—whereby he gets serious about giving up his besetting sin—he can finally begin to worship the Lord "in spirit and truth."

The issue of worship is strategically important in the war over occupation of the throne of a man's heart. His flesh loves sexual sin—that is inescapable. But what he can and must do is replace his love of sin with a consuming love

---

* As part of this, I would recommend an excellent book by Watchman Nee on the subject of brokenness entitled, *The Release of the Spirit.*
** A common mistake among addicts is to renounce what has been the object of their passion and to replace it with another seemingly more innocuous idol. This is only half-repentance.

for God. The answer is not simply hating the sin but learning to love and fear the Lord as well.

This brings us back to the examination of true worship. The man bound up in habits of immorality has allowed sexual pleasure to reign supreme in his heart. As with all idolatry, when a person worships something other than God, SELF becomes huge in his heart and the Lord becomes small. On the other hand, as he learns to bow before the Lord, God overshadows his inner being, and SELF diminishes. *True worship occurs only when the person sees who he is in relation to God and who God is in relation to him.* A great humbling can then take place, weakening the power of his flesh that loves the sin.

We must help the man see that true repentance is possible only when he is broken over his sinful, despicable condition and falls UNDONE at the feet of a holy God. There, prostrate before Calvary's cross, he is in right relationship with God and freed from the bondage of sin. Years of spiritual defeat now behind him, he can begin putting his sexuality in its proper place, and, most importantly, start loving God with all his heart, soul, and mind. He truly learns to worship Him "in spirit and truth."

THE PLACE OF DEVOTIONS

A believer's devotional life is of extreme importance in the development of a proper relationship with God. I won't take time here to address the nuts-and-bolts of establishing a daily time with the Lord as I have covered many of these issues in *At the Altar of Sexual Idolatry.* However, for the sake of reinforcing its value, I will touch upon a few of the benefits provided by a strong devotional life.

First of all, prayer helps the believer rise above the carnal life of the natural man. Walking in the Spirit requires a systematic and consistent prayer life. This is of immense import to the man in habitual sin. Paul gave what essentially amounts to a conditional promise when he said, "If you walk in the Spirit you will not fulfill the desires of the flesh." Brokenness is the entrance into the Spirit-led life; humble prayer is what maintains it.

The Word of God provides the necessary nourishment for maintaining spiritual health. Humans inherently need the influence of Scripture for personal growth. The man in habitual sin cannot hope to escape his carnal lifestyle and twisted perspectives on sexuality without a substantial dosage of the Bible everyday. However, if he spends time in it on a regular basis, God's thoughts will gradually replace his carnal mindset.

Establishing a habit of prayer and Bible reading also contributes to a disciplined lifestyle. One of the man's chief problems has been a life without restraint. Solomon rightly said, "*Like* a city that is broken into *and* without walls is a man who has no control over his spirit." (Proverbs 25:28) The discipline of getting up earlier in the morning to seek the Lord helps bring order to his otherwise chaotic existence.

Lastly, another benefit of spending time with the Lord is an increase of love and reverence for Him. It is impossible to love someone you do not know and equally impossible to know someone you are rarely around. The love of sexual sin can only be supplanted from the throne of a person's heart by an already existing love for God.

The essence of victorious Christianity hinges upon a person's relationship with the Almighty. This relationship must be nurtured if it is to grow. If neglected, it will wither away. This is a key element in helping a man find victory over habitual sin. Moreover, it is the crux of Christianity and should be the fundamental and essential goal of counseling.

three

THE METHOD OF OUR COUNSEL

Who could ever forget November 11, 2000, when the entire presidential election came down to the state of Florida? George W. Bush was eventually declared the winner of that state—and of the presidential race. However, Al Gore's attorneys appealed to the liberal Florida Supreme Court, coaxing them to write new laws in their favor that would give them the election. In the meantime, Democratic "spin-doctors" made the rounds on television talk shows attempting to incite a public outcry over the "terrible injustice" that had occurred. They created such a cloud of confusion that the average American completely lost sight of the fact that there are existing laws in place to deal with such matters.

Eventually, the United States Supreme Court stepped into the brouhaha and in essence said, "Wait a minute. You cannot just make new laws for the sake of convenience. It does not matter what is the current public opinion. Polls have no relevance in such matters. Dan Rather's opinion does not make a difference. The only determining factor in this is what is written in the Constitution." Thank God we have an

immovable legal charter that establishes rock-solid guidelines about how to run our nation! If it weren't for the Constitution, every decision lawmakers faced would be continually subject to the whims of the current pop culture.

In the same way, when it comes to determining the best
course of action for a believer struggling with sin, it is imperative that the counselor uses the Word of God—not simply as the ultimate authority on such matters—but also as an
actual handbook of solutions.

THE FORMATION OF AN ADDICTION

There are many teachings abounding today regarding
sexual addiction. As the field of psychology has evolved over
the past century, a great deal of speculation has taken place
regarding childhood development and its involvement in the
formation of emotional problems. In my book, *Irresistible to
God*, I wrote about how pride develops in a child.

Humans are born with a deeply felt need to be
loved and respected. This desire runs so deep that
the lack of noticeable appreciation by others—especially immediate family members—can actually be
emotionally damaging to a young child. A child's dependence upon the approval of others or his need
for affirmation often creates an overwhelming sense
of insecurity...

This so-called "inferiority complex" is reinforced
each time he experiences rejection or is emotionally hurt
in some way. The more inferior the child is made to feel
by the rejection of others, the more he will attempt to
compensate for that lack of security by exalting himself above others and protecting himself from their

41

put-downs. The child will often seek something—any-thing—to distinguish himself from others.

Consequently as a child develops, several things begin to happen. Certain forms of pride begin to surface within him in conjunction with his individu-ality: his strengths, abilities, looks, etc. If he is a sen-sitive person by nature, he will display self-protec-tive pride to ward off any pain or rejection by oth-ers. If he is naturally cocky, on the other hand, he will tend to be conceited and arrogant. The level of his insecurity—his thwarted desire to be highly thought of—usually determines the strength of his pride. Like sin of any kind, pride creates a down-ward spiral of soul degradation. The more one gives over to pride, the more that pride demands. In other words, it strengthens itself.

The child—who is only doing what comes natu-rally—gradually develops defense mechanisms to cope with being hurt in life. Unfortunately, these de-fense mechanisms are the embryos of pride that be-gin in childhood, are developed in the teen years, and are perfected in adulthood.

In the meantime, the youngster is completely unaware that he is a prime target of demonic spirits. These devils are very familiar with his family tree and all the different personality traits, secret sins, ar-eas of selfishness, and so on. In fact, these agents of darkness have been nurturing sin and pride in mem-bers of his family long before he was even born. As the child grows and suffers the inevitable pains of childhood, undoubtedly demons are present to show him how to respond to this pain. *Pride is the devil's solution to emotional pain.* In a fallen, sin-cursed world in which the pride of man is exalted, this ungodly attitude is carefully cultivated as the young person grows into adulthood.[1]

Although this segment refers to pride—that self-exalting attitude that afflicts every human—the same principles often apply to the formation of other sinful habits. Undoubtedly, childhood pain can set a young person on a course of seeking acceptance through sexual experiences, but this does not negate responsibility for his actions. Anywhere along the way he can turn to the Lord, rather than to sin. Furthermore, although the lack of emotional nurturing can play a part in the young person turning to sexual sin, let's not forget that illicit sex is a form of extreme pleasure. Ultimately and primarily, a person becomes addicted to sex because he has chosen to live a carnal life and yields to the cravings of his demanding flesh.

GETTING TO THE HEART OF THE PROBLEM

In an attempt to provide compassionate help to those who suffer from addictions, the secular field of psychotherapy has provided a plethora of answers to this dilemma. Nearly every teacher from the world of psychology views sexual addiction as an emotionally based problem. As such, a person's feelings and emotions become the focal point of all treatment. By and large, Christian psychologists take the same stance, adding the spiritual dynamic as a secondary issue. Although the counselee is taught to follow biblical teachings, he is told that his primary help will come as a result of his damaged emotions being treated by a professional.

Unquestionably, damaged emotions can play a part in the formation of a sexual addiction. However, it should never be forgotten that people sin because they have a fallen nature that is bent toward sin. The Bible never deals with such subjects from an emotional level. Actually, Scripture always approaches sin as a heart issue. Jeremiah summed up the problem when he wrote, "The heart is deceitful above all things and beyond cure. Who can understand it?" (Jeremiah 17:9 NIV) This statement exposes the human heart as the true culprit of sin.

Scripture also teaches that the heart is the center of man's being. Springing forth from that central location are one's attitudes, motives, feelings and emotions. One way to illustrate this is to think of the inner man as an underground spring, the heart being the source. David said, "...the inward thought and the heart of a man are deep." (Psalms 64:6) Solomon wrote, "Watch over your heart with all diligence, for from it flow the springs of life." (Proverbs 4:23)

If a dead carcass lying at the bottom has poisoned the water in that spring, it will not solve the problem to skim the foul scum off the top. The corpse must be withdrawn, and the spring must be flushed out.

As mankind's Creator (Colossians 1:16), Jesus is the ultimate authority on man's problems. He clearly laid out the source of sin when He said, "That which proceeds out of the man, that is what defiles the man. For from within, out of the heart of men, proceed the evil thoughts, fornications, thefts, murders, adulteries, deeds of coveting and wickedness, as well as deceit, sensuality, envy, slander, pride and foolishness. All these evil things proceed from within and defile the man." (Mark 7:20-23)

GOD'S METHOD OF DEALING WITH SIN

Undoubtedly, childhood trauma plays a part in the development of habitual sin. However, spending months wallowing in the quagmire of a man's past will not help him find freedom. As biblical counselors, our main concern is to lead the individual into a life of victory and godliness. Our primary question should not be, "How did this come about?" Rather, our main question is: "What does the Bible show us about how *God* deals with it?" An examination of Scripture reveals that the Lord has established a clear and predictable means of addressing human problems.

Throughout the entire breadth of Scripture, the Lord has consistently handled sin in the same manner. When Adam and Eve ate of the fruit, God immediately admonished them. When the children of Israel sinned in the wilderness, Moses rebuked them. When King Saul rebelled, the prophet Samuel confronted him. When David fell with Bathsheba, Nathan challenged him. Throughout the rest of the history of Israel, one sees God consistently respond to sin and rebellion by reproving the people through the prophets.

When Christ came to earth, He confronted nearly everybody He encountered. In fact, Jesus told His disciples, "If your brother sins, go and reprove him." (Matthew 18:15) Even the apostle Paul—the great champion of grace—continually confronted the sin of those to whom he ministered.

The inescapable fact is that the Lord never coddles sin. In a misguided sense of compassion, many often blameshift, minimize or explain away sin in the lives of counselees. Although God is exceedingly patient and full of grace, He is very unambiguous about His hatred of sin. Indeed, He has such an abhorrence of it that He sent His Son to die on the cross so that people could be freed from its tyranny. God is ruthless in His dealings with sin because it destroys the lives of those whom He greatly loves.

COUNSELING THE SINNER

As Paul was giving his farewell to the Ephesian elders, he said, "Remember that night and day for a period of three years, I did not cease to admonish each one with tears." (Acts 20:31) This statement is very enlightening because it gives insight into how he helped people during his stay in Ephesus.

The Greek word for admonish (*noutheteo*) which Paul employed here is defined as: "The verb means to impart understanding, to set right, to lay on the heart. The stress is on influencing not merely the intellect, but the will and disposition. The word thus acquires such senses as 'to admonish, to warn, to remind, and to correct.'"[2]

This term has become the flagstone of biblical counseling (sometimes referred to as *nouthetic* counseling). Although the problems people face can often be very complex, the biblical counselor's approach is to systematically work through and resolve the different issues people are confronted with. Most emotional problems people encounter are caused either as a direct result of sin in their lives or as an unbiblical response to the sin of others. In another work I told a story that highlights the way biblical counseling works:

The life of James Kenworth* is a classic example of someone whose problems were exacerbated by psychotherapeutic treatments. Plagued from childhood with social awkwardness, James became increasingly more detached from those around him as he grew into his teen years. His deep-seated fears limited his ability to interact with the other children at school. As he grew older he began dabbling in

---

* A pseudonym.

pornography, which caused him to withdraw even more. During his early twenties, he went regularly for counseling and attended twelve-step groups. After two years of this, his problems became so overwhelming his parents sent him to a Christian treatment center where anti-depressants were tried as a cure. Five weeks after leaving that facility he attempted suicide. His parents rushed him to the leading sexual addiction treatment center in the world. When they came to visit him several weeks later, they were shocked to find him curled up in a ball, holding a teddy bear. With his medical insurance about to run out, the staff began looking for another place to send him. Someone mentioned Pure Life Ministries.

The first day at Pure Life's live-in facility, he abruptly left the church service and ran down the street. Nevertheless, the biblical counselors at Pure Life brought him back and began working with him. He had always been told that he was a victim, but for the first time in his life, he accepted responsibility for his actions. The counselors required him to maintain a daily regimen of Bible study and prayer and to treat others with kindness. They told him, "You must live out in your daily life what the Bible teaches you should do." James faced tremendous battles with his flesh and with his thinking, but his counselors always provided encouragement and showed him patience and love. He began to respond almost immediately. Within weeks, he was a new person. Jesus Christ had come into his dark inner world and completely transformed him. It took a couple of years for him to work through some of his issues, but the fact is that he owes his soundness of mind to Jesus Christ alone.

His story is a case in point, which illustrates the difference between psychotherapy and biblical counseling. The one pampered him, using futile techniques and human pity which encouraged victim mentality and large-scale blameshifting. The other confronted him in a loving way about the selfishness of *his* sin. When he had viewed himself as a victim, he felt hopeless. When he saw that the problem was of his own making and that he needed to repent, immediately he saw also the way out. In other words, instead of being furnished with excuses for his behavior, he was required to take responsibility for his actions. He was pointed to Jesus Christ who is the only answer to the problems we have created for ourselves, even if others contributed to those problems. James discovered that Jesus never disappoints the seeking heart. His testimony is an irrefutable testimony to what God can do in a person's life who is willing to obey."[3]

True biblical counseling rests upon the standards Scripture imposes upon the life of the believer. A godly, loving counselor will patiently work with a man and help him to live up to the model of Christian life prescribed by the Bible. There is nothing mysterious about it. As the person begins to obey the Word of God, ungodly attitudes, perspectives and even desires all begin to change. Not only does the Bible supply the answers to man's problems, but it is also the very instrument the counselor uses as he works with him.

four

THE TOOL OF OUR COUNSEL

The Bible predicts that the last days will be a time of great lawlessness. This lack of respect for God's Word creates a moral atmosphere where sin can flourish. What happened in New York City during the 1980s is a good illustration of this. Violent crime was at epidemic levels when Mayor Guilianni came into office. He sized up the situation and quickly realized that there was a prevailing lack of respect for authority that had to be rectified before the crime rate could be substantially reduced. He ordered the NYPD to begin enforcing all of the laws—even minor violations such as jaywalking. He also cleaned out all of the adult bookstores, strip clubs and massage parlors from the Times Square section of Manhattan. Considering how overloaded the police department was already in handling major crimes, many ridiculed his strategy.

However, to the astonishment of supporters and critics alike, the crime rate immediately dropped! The truth he tapped into is that when a lawless attitude is prevalent within the general population, the amount of major crime will increase. Likewise, when people are taught to respect the law, the number of felonies committed will diminish.

This principle holds true for spiritual laws as well. Why is sexual sin running rampant within the Church? It is because we have lost our respect for the authority of God's Word in our lives. So, one of the first things the biblical counselor must establish in his own life is a love and respect for Scripture. As he himself learns to live what is taught in the Bible, he will be more equipped to instruct others to do the same. The effectiveness of his counsel to others will be directly proportioned to the reality of the Word of God in his own life.

The Word of God has much to say to the person caught in habitual sin. This divinely inspired tool has been furnished, but the Lord also needs "the workman who does not need to be ashamed, handling accurately the word of truth." (II Timothy 2:15) Paul shared with Timothy, his young protégé, the different ways Scripture might be used to help others:

> All Scripture is inspired by God and profitable for teaching, for reproof, for correction, for training in righteousness; that the man of God may be adequate, equipped for every good work... For the time will come when they will not endure sound doctrine; but *wanting* to have their ears tickled, they will accumulate for themselves teachers in accordance to their own desires; and will turn away their ears from the truth, and will turn aside to myths. (II Timothy 3:16-4:4)

Let us look at these four vital principles and how they apply in a practical sense to helping men bound in habitual sin.

TEACHING THE WORD

Imagine your typical counseling session. On the desk in front of you is God's Holy Word. Sitting across the desk from you is a man whose life has been ravaged by disobedience to that Word. You must convey to him the importance of explicitly following God's instructions for life that are contained therein.

Most likely your first challenge will be that this man has a much exaggerated opinion of his level of spirituality. In other words, although he has accumulated a lot of information about Christianity (i.e. head knowledge), he is actually living out only a very small percentage of what he has learned. Thus, you must lovingly help him to come into reality concerning his true spiritual state. Having him write out a testimony about what his Christian experience has been and a complete accounting of his current struggles will give you plenty of "ammunition" at your disposal as you begin showing him where he really is as a believer.

The truth is that—although he may have been a Christian for many years and possibly can quote Scripture ad infinitum—he is a baby believer and must be taken back to the basics of Christianity. He must be taught how—in a practical way—to live what is written in Scripture. What does it mean to his life to lay up treasures in heaven rather than on earth? How will it look in his life to actually learn to love others as he loves himself? How can he begin to see the faults in the lives of others through eyes of love, instead of through "haughty eyes?"

He must also be taught how to live in victory over sin. Teaching this man biblical principles will help to establish within him a mindset that will guide him as you work with him in the coming weeks. He will see the path to freedom from sexual sin laid before him in my book *At the Altar of Sexual Idolatry*, which gives a systematic accounting of what the Bible teaches on this subject.

REPROOF

Scripture establishes the parameters of a believer's life, and it is important to educate one's sheep about those restrictions. However, "Christian" sex addicts have established a pattern of picking and choosing when they will obey the Word. The man across from you clearly needs something stronger than a teaching from a book or sermon. He needs personal help.

Jesus spoke of the narrow path, which is simply a course of life delineated by biblical guidelines. Occasionally, believers veer off course for a variety of reasons. Indeed, this tendency is one of the very reasons Jesus had to go to the Cross: "All of us like sheep have gone astray, each of us has turned to his own way." (Isaiah 53:5) Left unchecked, many will continue to stray until they have completely fallen away from God in their hearts. Solomon said, "The backslider in heart will have his fill of his own ways..." (Proverbs 14:14)

As spiritual mentors, one of our tasks is to do everything within our power to keep this from happening to those to whom we minister. This drifting off-course occurs in many different ways. Even those who truly walk with God will have those times that they inwardly get away from the Lord.

I remember a time several years ago when Jeff Colon, the director of the Pure Life Ministries residential program, was struggling spiritually. This is certainly understandable. Living on site with 50 men seeking freedom from sexual sin is extremely draining. It's easy to get worn out and off-track. I could see that Jeff was in trouble, but I wasn't quite sure how to handle the situation. One morning the Lord laid it on my heart to confront him. I told him that it was obvious that he was sliding away from God in his heart. I strongly warned him that he needed to get himself back on track spiritually. It was a sobering wake-up call. He told me later, "I didn't even realize it at the time, but looking back, I can see that if I would have kept going in the direction I was headed, I very easily could have fallen into sin. Thank you so much!" His response was just what Solomon said it would be: "Reprove a wise man, and he will love you." (Proverbs 9:8)

Another situation in which men need to be confronted is when they begin to pursue sin. In one's spiritual journey occasionally there will be strong temptations that will crop up along the way. Solomon paints a vivid picture of the young man who runs into a beautiful prostitute in the street: "With her many persuasions she entices him; with her flattering lips she seduces him. Suddenly he follows her, as an ox goes to the slaughter..." (Proverbs 7:21-22) This is a picture of a man being baited into sexual sin.* Every step he takes leads him further into the insanity that accompanies sexual sin.

When the man of God sees his counselee going astray, he steps between him and the source of his temptation and in passionate, godly love says, "No! You can't do that!" He is, in essence, stopping this man from going over a spiritual cliff. This is biblical reproof. "...if another Christian is overcome by some sin, you who are godly should gently and humbly help that person back onto the right path..."

---

* There was a time when we used to raise and butcher our own cattle at the PLM facility. We would lay down a trail of corn on the ground, which would lead the young steer to the spot we had chosen to slaughter him. It was an amazing picture of how Satan tantalizes a man toward the place where he can spring his trap on him.

God has inspired Scripture for this very purpose. The counselor has been given the authority to reprove this man by the guidelines and mandates it has established. This is very important for the "Christian" sex addict who has a pattern of selective obedience. The counselor who uses this tool sparingly and lovingly will find it to be absolutely lifesaving for some. A timely rebuke will spare some people from a lifetime of suffering. "He is on the path of life who heeds instruction, but he who forsakes reproof goes astray." (Proverbs 10:17)

CORRECTION

The corrupting effects of sin upon the human mind should never be underestimated. Sin has the power to alter a person's perspectives, values and attitudes. One of the reasons it is imperative that a believer maintains a vibrant devotional life is because he so desperately needs the constant influence of God's perspectives upon his mind.

When the biblical counselor starts working with a man in habitual sin, he soon discovers that there are many areas of his life that do not line up with Scripture. Correction is there for the purpose of helping to guide the counselee back into biblical thinking and living. Teaching establishes the boundaries established by Scripture. Reproof is occasionally used when a man veers off track. Correction contains elements of both of these. It is setting the "broken bones" of the man's soul. It is helping him to get his thinking untwisted.

TRAINING

Our final term (Gk. *paideia*) is used only four other times in Scripture—three in the same chapter. I will provide these verses to give a better comprehension for what this word means:

- And, fathers, do not provoke your children to anger; but bring them up in the discipline (*paideia*) and instruction of the Lord. (Ephesians 6:4)
- ...My son, do not regard lightly the discipline (*paideia*) of the Lord... (Hebrews 12:5)
- It is for discipline (*paideia*) that you endure; God deals with you as with sons; for what son is there whom *his* father does not discipline (*paideuo*)? (Hebrews 12:7)
- All discipline (*paideia*) for the moment seems not to be joyful, but sorrowful; yet to those who have been trained by it, afterwards it yields the peaceful fruit of righteousness. (Hebrews 12:11)

The verb form of this word used in Hebrews 12:7 (*paideuo*) is the same word Pilate employed when speaking of Jesus: "I will therefore *punish* Him and release Him." (Luke 22:16) Translators were correct to apply the term "training" here, but it must be understood that it contains within it a stronger sense than one would typically think. There is an element of authority that is connected to this word: father-son, God-believer and even Pilate-criminal (Jesus).

Training involves one person building into the life of another. Teaching tends to be impersonal and vague, such as preaching on a particular subject to an entire congregation or even giving a counselee a book to read. Training, on the other hand, is very personal and specific.

I must include in here a word of caution to pastors. While the pulpit is the perfect vehicle for teaching important truths to the entire congregation from the Word of God, it will only accomplish so much in their lives. There is a reason

God has provided ministers with four ways to use Scripture. If a pastor only teaches and neglects the other three tools at his disposal, his ministry will only be operating at one-fourth its power! Can you imagine a four-cylinder engine firing on a single cylinder? It would struggle along, "spitting and coughing." If people are to be effectively helped through their struggles, someone must get his hands dirty! Somebody must be willing to get involved in the lives of individuals.

IN RIGHTEOUSNESS

I am not a Greek scholar, but I don't think I would be too far off base grammatically to suggest that this last term should be coupled with all four usages of the Bible—not simply the word training. In other words, Scripture is inspired by God and profitable for *teaching* in righteousness, for *reproof* in righteousness, for *correction* in righteousness, and for *training* in righteousness.

The term righteousness primarily has to do with the way believers treat others: having a concern about the rights of other people. One teacher called it "the other guy's bill of rights." For instance, did you know that six of the Ten Commandments have to do with the way we interact with other people? Even the first four Commandments revolve around the manner we behave toward God.

Rest assured that the man in habitual sexual sin is routinely trouncing upon the rights of God, family members, friends and others. The counselor will help him by teaching him what the Bible says about godly living, reproving him when he strays off course, correcting sinful thinking and training him in how to live a life which pleases God. All of this is designed to help the man learn how to live righteously before God and man. The Bible is "God-breathed" for the purpose of helping people. No wonder David said, "The Law of the Lord is perfect, restoring the soul." (Psalm 19:7) It inherently contains all that is needed to bring restoration to the wayward soul.

USING CHURCH DISCIPLINE

The Word of God is not only the source of our counsel, but it is also the tool we use to help men escape the insane thinking that sin produces and come into the Lord's mindset. We have seen the wonderful ways Scripture can be used to help the man bound in habitual sin: teaching, reproof, correction, and training. This all falls under the category of discipleship.

But what happens when a man does not apply biblical teaching? What do you do when he rejects your attempts to reprove or correct him? How do you handle it when he does not respond to your training? If you care about him, you must take the process to the next level.

The Bible is very practical and provides solutions to this sort of dilemma. Jesus said, "And if your brother sins, go and reprove him in private; if he listens to you, you have won your brother. But if he does not listen *to you,* take one or two more with you, so that by the mouth of two or three witnesses every fact may be confirmed. And if he refuses to listen to them, tell it to the church; and if he refuses to listen even to the church, let him be to you as a Gentile and a tax-gatherer." (Matthew 18:15-17) In these few statements, He wisely laid down a systematic course of action one can take to help the resistant believer. It takes place in four steps:

- Reprove in private
- Reprove with two witnesses

- Bring the sin before the entire church
- Treat the sinner as an unbeliever

The process begins with reproof (Gk. *elegcho*), the very same term used by Paul in the passage we have examined in this chapter. Jesus later made the statement, "Those whom I love, I reprove and discipline..." (Revelation 3:19) As we have already observed, reproof is an important aspect of effective ministry. However, in one sense, the way Jesus uses the term in regards to church discipline actually encompasses all four of the tools mentioned earlier.* In other words, the minister has been using the four-fold method of working with the man outlined above. Nevertheless, the man does not seem to be taking his sin seriously.

At this point stronger measures are in order. Jesus says that we must now reprove him with "two witnesses." This statement refers back to the Old Testament economy when two or three witnesses were required to convict a man of wrongdoing. (Deuteronomy 19:15) In the New Testament context, this should include church elders or pastors.

There is a very good reason for doing this. Bringing more people into the counseling setting tends to intensify the seriousness of the situation in the erring brother's mind. Having two church elders present will give the man a sense of the gravity of his sin. Countless times over the years I have seen this wake-up call bring a man to true repentance.

Unfortunately, sometimes even this does not accomplish the desired effect. "And if he refuses to listen to them," Jesus goes on to say, "tell it to the church." Up to this point, his privacy has been carefully protected, but once the pastor

---

* The primary usage of reproof used here by Jesus refers to rebuking a man over an offensive pattern of sin.

begins to sense that the man is refusing the correction, he is instructed to bring the sin into the light for all to see. Now the situation is treated with even more gravity. This man's future (and possibly even his eternity) is at stake! He needs to wake up! Perhaps the shame of being exposed before the entire church will be enough to help him repent.

However, Jesus goes on to say, "if he refuses to listen even to the church, let him be to you as a Gentile and a tax-gatherer." This is the last step to reach the erring brother. This may seem extreme, but God takes drastic measures whenever there is an unrepentant sinner in the camp. (Joshua 7; Acts 5) Dr. Jay Adams said, "No one should be put out of the church because of his sin (as though some sins require discipline and others do not). No, precisely not that. It is the failure to 'hear' that moves discipline to the final stage of putting one out of your midst."[1]

We find an example of this in First Corinthians 5 where a man was living in sin with his father's wife. In this instance the man needed to be brought to the final stage of church discipline quickly: "Remove the wicked man from among yourselves," Paul told the church.

THE GOALS OF CHURCH DISCIPLINE

Without a doubt it takes a great deal of courage for a pastor in our day and age to excommunicate an unrepentant sinner. Not only must the pastor face the man's anger, but the members of his church may misunderstand his intentions. Nevertheless, there are three very important reasons why it must be done.

First, the spiritual integrity of the church must be maintained. Paul said, "Clean out the old leaven, that you may be a new lump..." (I Corinthians 5:7) Leaven illustrates the contagious and corrupting power of sin. A church that is tolerant of sin will soon be full of compromise.

Second, when someone in sin is dealt with openly, it causes the other members of the Body to comprehend the seriousness of sin. Paul told Timothy, "Those who continue in sin, rebuke in the presence of all, so that the rest also may be fearful of sinning." (I Timothy 5:20) This seems to be a forgotten concept in many of today's "seeker-friendly" churches.

Third, it is done to save an unrepentant sinner from his sin. Paul told the Corinthians, "I have decided to deliver such a one to Satan for the destruction of his flesh, that his spirit may be saved in the day of the Lord Jesus." We must remember that God is more concerned about a person's eternal destiny than He is about his temporary comfort. If a person refuses to repent, the time will come when God will "give them over" to their sin. (Romans 1:24, 26) This happened to the man in Corinth, and we find out later that he repented of his sin. (II Corinthians 2:6-8) The complete restoration of an erring believer is the ultimate goal of church discipline.

Is there a place in 21st century Christianity for church discipline? Absolutely! Our loving Savior has been in the business of correcting wayward souls for a long time. In spite of the fact that we may not understand what the Lord is doing, we may rest assured in the knowledge that He has a definite purpose in mind for all His dealings with His children. It is the Word of God that provides the authority to teach, counsel and discipline.

five

THE GOAL OF OUR COUNSEL

In his book, *Leaving Yesterday Behind*, my friend Bill Hines tells two stories in the final chapter that are very pertinent to the issues we are examining. He first relates a conversation he had with a former counselee who felt disappointed and unhappy as a believer. Dr. Hines asked her, "Did you become a Christian because of how it made you feel or did you become a Christian because Christianity is true?"

The second story is about a man who sought to divorce his wife because he no longer felt love for her. The author, again as counselor, said to him, "You seem to place the emphasis on being happy. Is that what you see as the goal of your life?" In true J.F.K. fashion,* Dr. Hines concluded his book with the statement: "if you want to have the break with your past that really means something for all eternity... you must stop asking, 'How can I be happy?' and begin asking, 'How can I make God happy?'"[1] A.W. Tozer made this same point when he said, "God is not concerned about our

---

* "Ask not what your country can do for you, but ask what you can do for your country!"

happiness but our holiness." In other words, the ultimate purpose of the believer's life should not be the pursuit of temporary happiness but rather an undying passion to please God.

Consequently, as biblical counselors, our primary goal must be to help our counselees mature spiritually so that they might exhibit this quality of life.

THE IMPORTANCE OF GOALS

When I was in my early twenties, I worked as a real estate salesman for a couple of years. During that time I listened to a series of talks given by Earl Nightingale, a motivational speaker. One of the principles he emphasized is that in order to be successful at your work, you must keep the image of success before your eyes as much as possible. However, since success can be such a vague concept, he recommended mounting pictures on the wall of tangible signs of success (i.e. a new car, a custom home, etc.). Although I later renounced this entire hedonistic mindset, I realized that Nightingale had stumbled upon a legitimate principle of life: if a person is going to work, he must know what he is working toward. By the same token, without a clear-cut objective in view, people tend to aimlessly wander through life oblivious to God's will for them.

I can illustrate the truth of this from another period of my life. When I founded Pure Life Ministries in 1986, God gave me a clear vision of an organization that would one day have a national (and even international) scope. It seemed that this lofty aspiration would quickly come to fruition after a number of appearances on national television and radio programs. After about three years of this exposure, the Lord led Kathy and me to relocate the ministry to Kentucky. We purchased a house on some acreage and opened our home to minister to sexual addicts. In the meantime, all the media doors that had been wide open to me during the Bakker and Swaggart fiascos closed. Producers were no longer interested in having me as a guest on their programs.

For the next ten years we languished on that farm. The vision I had received in 1986 was all but forgotten. We had lost our purpose. As we continued to help the men God sent to us, we did not realize at the time that God was behind the death of this vision. He used those hard years to do a deep work inside us that was desperately needed. Nevertheless, as we lost sight of our goal as an organization, we also lost our motivation to work. The ministry floundered until September 1999, when the Lord renewed the vision and directed us to work to fulfill it.*

Such aimlessness describes the daily existence of many believers today who travel on their Christian journey with no real direction or sense of destiny. They might occasionally hear some good teachings that temporarily motivate them, but there is no real purpose in their spiritual lives.** It's almost as if they are just sort of waiting to get raptured or die and go to heaven.

ESTABLISHING THE GOAL

When dealing with counselees, it is imperative to keep in front of them the goal they are working toward. The purpose of all true biblical counseling is found in Paul's words: "we proclaim Him, admonishing every man and teaching

---

* I should clarify that my personal goal of Christlikeness was never stronger than at this time.
** It seems that most believers have more concern with worldly aspirations than spiritual objectives.

every man with all wisdom…" (Colossians 1:28) Why? "that we may present every man complete in Christ." Simply put, the number one objective of every believer should be to think and act biblically—to become more Christlike.

The Greek word for complete that Paul used here to describe this wonderful aspiration is *teleios*, which means, "to accomplish, complete, consummate, fulfill, or make perfect." To help bring out its real meaning, I will provide three of its other usages in Scripture:

- Therefore you are to be *perfect*, as your heavenly Father is *perfect*. (Matthew 5:48)
- Therefore leaving the elementary teaching about the Christ, let us press on to *maturity*… (Hebrews 6:1)
- Consider it all joy, my brethren, when you encounter various trials, knowing that the testing of your faith produces endurance. And let endurance have *its perfect* result, that you may be *perfect* and complete, lacking in nothing. (James 1:2-4)

All three of these passages of Scripture express different aspects of the same thing: maturing spiritually and becoming more like Christ.

Undisputedly, Jesus was the greatest biblical counselor who ever lived.* His dealings with the various people He encountered can be described as nothing less than masterful. Many examples in the Gospels could be cited, but to show how He used this important term, I will briefly touch upon the occasion when the rich, young ruler approached Him. This earnest young man asked Him the most signifi-

---

* Isaiah 9:6.

cant, urgent question that anyone could ask. "Teacher, what good thing shall I do that I may obtain eternal life?" (Matthew 19:16) After a brief interchange with him, Jesus went right to the real issue in this man's heart: "If you wish to be complete (*teleios*), go and sell your possessions and give to the poor, and you shall have treasure in heaven; and come, follow Me."

Jesus, the Surgeon of souls, looked right into this man's inner being and saw something very foul and cancerous: covetousness. In one short statement He gave the man the needed solution: "If you want a healthy soul... If you desire your life to be pleasing to the Lord... If you wish to be spiritually mature... then repent of your greed, unshackle yourself from these possessions, and fill your life with God." As a biblical counselor, Jesus fulfilled His calling. He presented the necessary truth with love.* It was then up to the man to decide whether or not he would obey.

What a comfort to know that Jesus Himself is the *teleios* for every believer. He is "the hope of glory." Indeed, He was the most "together" person who has ever lived. Jesus possessed an astounding level of personal maturity. He did not carry around the emotional baggage that inevitably accompanies sin—He was *full* of the Holy Spirit. (Luke 4:1) Although He was called the "Man of Sorrows" (because He grieved over the hardheartedness of those He ministered to), He was also an extremely joyful person. Children would look into His face and find a gracious, inviting expression. It is this marvelous person whom we are called to emulate. His life epitomizes spiritual and emotional well-being.

---

* Mark 10:21.

WORKING TOWARD THE GOAL

One does not become Christlike automatically, simply because he has been a Christian for a long time. Becoming more like Jesus is a process by which the Holy Spirit changes the person inside. His perspectives, values, thought patterns and even desires become gradually altered. Paul described the new birth experience in this way: "Therefore if any man is in Christ, he is a new creature; the old things passed away; behold, new things have come." (II Corinthians 5:17) This goes along with another statement he made when he said, "...we have the mind of Christ." (I Corinthians 2:16) Many believers have doubted the veracity of these statements because the old ways of thinking—still so alive within them—makes them feel as though nothing as changed.

Before coming to Christ, every believer was "alienated and hostile in mind," toward God. (Colossians 1:21) However, when a man becomes born again, he suddenly comes under the influence of the Holy Spirit and has access to the mind of Christ. Although most of the old thought patterns are still intact through the force of habit, he now has the opportunity to work with God to displace his carnal mindset with a godly mind. (Romans 12:2) He is a new creature in the sense that he now has the Holy Spirit residing within him. Nevertheless, he must still cooperate with the Lord's work in his life for this transformation to occur. The Bible calls this process sanctification:

> *Progressive sanctification* describes the development of Christian character. It means to mature in the faith. As the new believer, full of self and all its baggage of sin, pride, and selfishness, undergoes the sanctifying processes of God, he gradually conforms to the likeness

of Christ. Sanctification is *how* a person is made holy. It is the *process*; holiness is the *result*. Paul refers to progressive sanctification when he says that believers are "predestined to become conformed to the image of His Son. . ." (Romans 8:29) and "are being transformed into the same image from glory to glory..." (II Corinthians 3:18) It is what he was referring to when he says, "Do not be conformed to this world, but be transformed by the renewing of your mind. . ." (Romans 12:2) Or in the words of Peter, becoming "partakers of the divine nature, having escaped the corruption that is in the world by lust." (II Peter 1:4) Holiness is to the soul what health is to the physical body: freedom from the damaging effects of impurity.[2]

TEARING DOWN THE OLD

The Bible employs different terminology to describe how this process actually occurs within a believer's life. In Colossians 3, Paul wrote: "Put to death, therefore, whatever belongs to your earthly nature: sexual immorality, impurity, lust, evil desires and greed, which is idolatry." (Colossians 3:5 NIV) In Galatians 5, he explained: "Now those who belong to Christ Jesus have crucified the flesh with its passions and desires." (Galatians 5:24) In Ephesians 4, he said it this way: "You were taught, with regard to your former way of life, to put off your old self, which is being corrupted by its deceitful desires; to be made new in the attitude of your minds; and to put on the new self, created to be like God in true righteousness and holiness." (Ephesians 4:22-24) Although the terminology differs, in each case the reader is challenged to replace past behavior patterns with new ones by emulating Christ. This is all simply another way of exhorting people to repent of (i.e. to change their mind about) everything in their lives that keeps them from God.

In many instances, the Bible makes an analogy between a house and a person's life (cf. Matthew 7, I Corinthians 3, II Corinthians 5, II Timothy 2, I Peter 2). This same comparison could also describe the process of sanctification. Imagine visiting an affluent neighborhood in West Los Angeles. Street after street boasts spectacular mansions with perfectly manicured lawns. You drive through the area in wide-eyed astonishment. Suddenly you come upon a shack, sandwiched in between two palatial estates. The grandeur of the other homes in the area only augments the shabbiness of this out of place shanty.

That dilapidated house is a picture of a person's old nature. When Jesus is allowed into a person's life, He immediately begins dismantling that old shack plank by plank. Jesus is a carpenter and He shows up with crowbars, sledgehammers and skill-saws. As soon as He begins prying boards loose, the man often panics. In a last ditch effort to salvage what remains, he tacks up a few boards and paints the weathered, cracked exterior. In his opinion, it looks better than it ever has. This rundown house may not look as nice as other places, but it is all this man has. To him, it seems cruel of Jesus to want to tear it completely down.

If that were all Jesus purposed to do, it would be a mean thing to do indeed. However, what the man does not realize is that an entire construction crew is headed to his location. Just as soon as that old house is demolished, they are going to build him a multi-million dollar mansion fully furnished with everything brand new!*

---

* I should mention that many counseling methods are nothing more than an attempt to beautify the old man. The Self-Esteem Movement is one such example.

In the realm of humanism—where everything passes through the lens of a temporal mindset—biblical confrontation can seem unkind and condemning. "How can you tell that person that his life is displeasing to God?" some would ask incredulously. "He needs to be encouraged, not demoralized!" Of course there is a place for encouragement, but if this man does not come into reality about his godless life, he is doomed for destruction. Is it really merciful to simply encourage a man when he is walking toward a cliff?

Before anyone can experience a life of victory, he must embrace God's discipline. He must allow the Lord to begin dismantling his life of defeat. The end of this process is the blessed life of holiness. (Hebrews 12:5-11) This is where he will find victory. This is where he will find God.

THE NUTS AND BOLTS
OF OUR COUNSEL

In this section, we have dealt with some of the peripheral issues surrounding the process of counseling a man who is in habitual sexual sin. We began by describing the important role of the counselor's personal spiritual life. In the second chapter, we discussed the bottom line of Christianity: one's relationship with God. Having established that, Chapter Three focused on how to approach counseling biblically. After tackling that issue, we looked at the powerful role the Word of God plays in the entire process. Finally, in the last chapter we outlined the ultimate goal for the individual's life. We turn our attention now to the practical aspects of counseling.

How does a counselor actually help a man get from his current life of defeat into one of victory? Where does one begin such a monumental undertaking? What part does the counselor play in the individual's progress? These and other issues will be addressed in this chapter.

THE APPLICATION PROCESS

As part of the enrollment process for Pure Life Ministries' residential program, the potential student must fill out an extensive application. In addition, he is required to write a "testimony" of his spiritual experience, including the extent of his involvement in sexual sin. Upon reviewing this information, the program director then conducts a telephone interview. The purpose of this induction process is two-fold.

The first reason for this methodical application process, of course, is to determine whether or not the man is accepted into the program. As a matter of policy, we do not accept every applicant into our facility. This strategy comes directly from the Bible. Jesus said, "Do not give what is holy to dogs, and do not throw your pearls before swine, lest they trample them under their feet, and turn and tear you to pieces." (Matthew 7:6) In a certain way, Jesus was simply restating what Solomon had said nearly 1,000 years before: "He who corrects a scoffer gets dishonor for himself, and he who reproves a wicked man gets insults for himself. Do not reprove a scoffer, lest he hate you..." (Proverbs 9:7-8)* Notice that believers are *commanded* not to expend themselves upon those who will not respond to their efforts. Charles Spurgeon comments upon the Matthew passage:

> When men are evidently unable to perceive the purity of a great truth, do not set it before them. They are like a mere *dog,* and if you set holy things before them they will be provoked to *"turn again and rend you"*... do not bring forth the precious mysteries of the faith, for they will despise them, and *"trample them under their feet"* in the mire. You are not needlessly to provoke attack upon yourself, or upon the higher truths of the gospel.[1]

---

* It should be noted that Solomon used two important counseling terms here: correct and reprove.

In my early years of ministry, I learned through painful experience the truth conveyed in these passages of Scripture. As I ministered to numerous struggling men over the telephone, I soon realized that most were not heeding my counsel. Time after time, I poured myself into their lives, only to be disappointed by their lack of responsiveness to the Lord, or worse, their attacks. Gradually, I developed the conviction that we at PLM should do everything possible to weed out those who were not serious about achieving victory. Every minute spent on someone unwilling to respond to God, was a minute stolen away from a sincere seeker.

A counselor or minister only has a certain amount of time and energy he can devote to the lives of others. The fruit of his ministry depends upon him focusing his full attention on those who will truly benefit from it. Throughout the years, we have developed the following philosophy at PLM:

- Do our utmost to prayerfully determine a person's sincerity level.
- Do not spend our resources on those who seem insincere.
- Do everything within our power to help those who are sincere.

Some may consider this method lacking in compassion. Actually, this approach is very merciful. First, those who earnestly desire help receive the valuable resources they need. Second, those initially denied entry into our residential program may reapply later when they are more likely to take full advantage of the opportunity. We would rather deny a man entry to PLM in hopes that he reapplies later (when he is ready) than to see him fail the program and lose all hope.

The benefits of this philosophy at Pure Life have been enormous. Our policy of weeding out those unwilling to "jump through the hoops" has enabled us to pour all of our energies into those prepared to respond. This same principle can be applied in the context of counseling.

The second reason for the application process is to gather useful information about the counselee which, if he is accepted into the program, will serve several useful purposes in future counseling sessions:

First, the counselor will become acquainted with the man and his problems. The application will provide him with a number of useful facts: age, marital status, children, occupation, medical problems, and denominational background. His testimony will fill in a number of blanks about his Christian experience and the extent of his problems. Hopefully, he will share openly the areas of sexual sin he has been involved in: pornography, strip clubs, adultery, encounters with prostitutes, voyeurism, homosexuality, etc.

Not only will these tools provide such bare facts, but they will also communicate the man's perspectives on life, Christianity, and his own problems. Underlying attitudes will often surface as he shares his story. The counselor should ponder the following questions: Does he seem as though he has a lot of spiritual pride? To what degree is he in delusion over his sin? Is he blameshifting or taking responsibility for his own actions? Does he seem sincere in his efforts to change?

There is another way this information can be useful. Prior to entering the counseling process, the man is typically feeling the urgency of his need. His crisis has forced him to seek help from an outside source. Thus, it is likely that, in writing down his story, he is giving a fairly honest and detailed description of the depths and degree of his sin. Later, if he begins to minimize his problems, the counselor can actually read back to him his own words about the scope of his sin. Hopefully, this will serve as a wake-up call as he is faced with his former perspective on the extent of his sin.

Any counselor, minister or men's leader can utilize this application process. Counselees should be required to fill out an application and provide a detailed description of their spiritual lives and sexual struggles.

THE FIRST SESSION

Prior to the counselee's first visit, the counselor has already familiarized himself with the man and his problems by reviewing the application (and/or other data-gathering device). He has spent time praying over this man's dilemma, seeking God to provide insights and guidance during their first encounter. He enters this situation as prepared as is practically possible.

There are two things he should do to open the session, both of which establish the course of all future counseling. First, he ought to pray. This is an opportunity to ask God—in front of the man—for some important things to be accomplished. Additionally, he could ask the counselee to say a prayer of commitment to doing whatever is necessary to find the victory he is seeking.

The other thing that he should do is ask the man two simple questions: "Are you willing to accept the Bible as the source of authority for all counseling that takes place?" and "Are you willing to obey the Word of God to the best of your ability?" Most Christians will readily agree to these two stipulations. If, for any reason, the man is unwilling to consent to these conditions, then the session should be immediately terminated. As an explanation, the counselor might say, cannot have an established authority to work from, I'm afraid there is little I can do to help you."

Acceptance of these prerequisites not only establishes a biblical framework for all future counseling, but, if necessary, can also be an important tool for later use. For instance, let's say a month into the counseling a situation arises where the man is asked to obey a biblical commandment that he has previously avoided. The counselor can remind him of their initial agreement in the hopes of motivating him to do the right thing.

Once these two initial objectives have been met, the counselor can proceed with the actual session. There are two goals for this first encounter.

First, the counselor will ask pertinent questions that help shed more light on the exact nature of the problem. Listening is a crucial part of the counseling process.* A counselee will not trust a counselor who rushes to conclusions or does not take the time to hear his story. Solomon said, "He who gives an answer before he hears, it is folly and shame to him." (Proverbs 18:13)

The counselor should ask specific questions that will help to sharpen his understanding of the situation. Quality counseling always rests upon three legs: an accurate appraisal of the problem, the solution provided by God's Word, and the loving discipleship that will help the counselee live according to that solution. The use of pinpoint questioning that leaves no room for vague generalities is essential to arrive at

---

* There are two things I must interject here. First, in and of itself, talk is not therapeutic. It may make the counselee temporarily feel a sense of relief to express his innermost thoughts, but it does not, alone, provide help. Second, it is important that the counselor maintains control over the counseling session. Some counselees will ramble on aimlessly, talking about everything under the sun. This creates confusion within the counseling setting and promotes hopelessness.

a correct understanding of the man's struggle: "Exactly what kind of sexual behavior were you involved in?" "How many times a week would you typically act out?" "How often were other people involved in your activities?" This depth of detail proves beneficial later as the counselor offers concrete solutions to the various aspects of the problem.* These details should be carefully noted by the counselor for future reference.

The second goal of that first session should be establishing hope in the mind of the counselee. Earlier, we discussed the overwhelming sense of despair experienced by the typical Christian sexual addict. This hopelessness arises partially from the fact that he has been repeatedly given exaggerated promises by authors and teachers attempting to sell him their wares. Each time a purported solution proves ineffective, his hope for change further diminishes. As he continues in sin year after year, his futility mounts. Nothing destroys the promise of the future like habitual sin.

However, the good news for this man is that, regardless of his past experience, God's Word remains an eternal source of truth and surety. (Psalm 119:89) If he has failed to receive promised victory, it is because he himself has not fulfilled the conditions attached to that promise.

Be that as it may, hope tends to come through a pattern of structure. When a person aimlessly wanders through life (especially in the case of habitual sin), it is very easy for the future to seem bleak. However, when a definite course of action is laid out before him, a growing hope is birthed within him. Instead of an enormous mountain of sin looming in his sights, he can see a stairway going up and over that peak.

---

* I must interject a word of caution here. We want the counselee to be specific about his activities without sharing indecent and explicit details.

Accordingly, one of the first things the counselor should do is outline a game plan with the counselee. This may include a pre-determined number of sessions (which can be changed later, if need be), a required devotional time that steadily increases, and different types of homework. As this strategy is mapped out for the man, a growing sense of a "light at the end of the tunnel" intensifies within him. Rather than a vague, never-ending series of counseling sessions, he now has sight of a very attainable goal.

THE IMPORTANCE OF HOMEWORK

One of the vital aspects of all biblical counseling is homework. Counseling sessions alone provide a wonderful opportunity to work through the various issues that arise. However, the ultimate purpose of biblical counseling is complete transformation. This change comes about primarily as the person begins to live according to the mandates of Scripture. A life of obedience becomes one of the prime overall objectives. Talking about these biblical guidelines has its place, but it is important that the man actually begins to implement these changes in his daily life. Homework provides the necessary structure to do this.

Assignments can assume different forms. To illustrate, let's examine the case of a man who consistently takes his wife for granted. His lack of gratitude has caused problems in the marriage and contributed to his sexual sin (cf. *At the Altar of Sexual Idolatry*, Chapter Two). Throughout your time together, he works on this area of his life in various ways. At the end of one session, you ask him to list 40 things about his wife for which he is grateful. The following week you ask him to do a Bible study on the concept of thankfulness. You explain to him in as detailed a manner as possible that you want him to write out ten verses that pertain to this subject, including a short paragraph on how each verse relates to his life. He should provide personal application, not a running commentary! In a subsequent meeting, you ask him to personally express gratitude to his wife at least twice a day during the following week. He should document each occurrence and bring the results for discussion at the next counseling session. These are just a few examples of homework assignments that I have found very effective in helping a man change.

In his excellent work, *The Christian Counselor's Manual,*[2] Dr. Jay Adams lists six purposes accomplished through the use of homework. I will quote them verbatim and encapsulate what he wrote about each:

1. *"Regular homework assignments set a pattern for expectation of change."* By giving the counselee concrete things to do, he is establishing an environment conducive to change. Something more is expected of the man than mere talk. He must begin to change the way he actually lives his life.

2. *"Homework clarifies expectations."* Giving the counselee an assignment keeps the counseling very clear and concrete. It helps cut through confusion.

3. *"Homework enables the counselor to do more counseling more rapidly."* The counselee accomplishes much in between sessions by working on his homework. More time is then available during the actual sessions to focus on important topics.

4. *"Homework keeps counselees from becoming dependent*

upon the counselor." Homework tends to help the counselee see the Lord as his helper and His Word as the source of his answers.

5. *"Homework enables both the counselor and the counselee to gauge progress or lack of it."* "The proof is in the pudding," as the saying goes. Homework is a great way to determine a man's sincerity level. If he does not complete his assignments, it becomes obvious to both parties that he is not serious. Likewise, faithful application to the homework builds his confidence.

6. *"Homework allows the counselor to deal with problems and patterns that develop under controlled current conditions."* These assignments can be an effective device for gathering important data about the counselee and his current situation.

Consistent application of all available tools enables the counselor to be used by God to help those desperate for change. However, given the current state of America, counseling can be extremely unpredictable. In a society so inundated by pornographic images and saturated in perversion, the Christian who makes himself available to help others must be prepared to deal with a myriad of situations.

BOOK TWO

COUNSELING SPECIFICS

But you, beloved, building yourselves up on your most holy faith, praying in the Holy Spirit, keep yourselves in the love of God, waiting anxiously for the mercy of our Lord Jesus Christ to eternal life.

And have mercy on some, who are doubting; save others, snatching them out of the fire; and on some have mercy with fear, hating even the garment polluted by the flesh. Now to Him who is able to keep you from stumbling, and to make you stand in the presence of His glory blameless with great joy, to the only God our Savior, through Jesus Christ our Lord, *be* glory, majesty, dominion and authority, before all time and now and forever. Amen. (Jude 17-25) seven

COUNSELING YOUNG PEOPLE

Adults, unfortunately, are not the only ones affected by the escalation of perversity in this country. America's youth are being corrupted like never before. Not only are pornography usage and promiscuity at disturbingly high levels, but vast numbers of children are being molested each year as well. In one form or another, sexual sin is deeply affecting the lives of many of our young people. These damaged souls also need help.

Many of the problems they face regarding sexual sin can be handled in the same manner as when dealing with adults. However, there are certain issues that are distinctly theirs. While not exhaustively dealing with the sexual challenges encountered by today's young people, this chapter should provide the counselor with valuable insight into two crucial subjects: molestation victims and teenagers who habitually masturbate. These topics are herein addressed by articles recently published in *Unchained*, the Pure Life Ministries magazine.

Counseling Children
Who Have Been Molested

Cassie is the object of ridicule in her junior high school because she is overweight and has body odor. Her peers are unaware that she is subconsciously making herself unattractive to her stepfather who has been molesting her for the past three years.

At age 12, Jimmy is already abusing drugs and getting in trouble at school. His schoolmates are fearful of his violent temper. Jimmy's deep-seated anger stems from being molested by his uncle.

Much too young to be thinking of such things, 13-year-old Beth has already had sex with a number of boys from school. She, like her older sister, was molested by their stepfather. Following in the footsteps of her older sister, who is now a stripper, she has learned to attract boys by wearing revealing clothes.

Heather lives in a constant state of fear and is riddled with guilt. Her daddy has been molesting her off and on for the past five years. On a number of occasions he has told her that if she ever reports him he'll be thrown in jail. Consequently, she keeps it a secret and bears the responsibility of keeping the family unit intact.

Seventeen-year-old Ben has become cold and sullen. He puts up walls, refusing to make himself vulnerable to others. He also suffers from insomnia because nighttime was when his older stepbrother used to slip into his room to molest him.

Unquestionably, sin destroys lives. Perhaps there is no sin that leaves such devastation in its wake as that of child abuse. Long after an offender has indulged his perverted fantasies, the effects of his actions continue to haunt the child. One moment of lust can produce a lifetime of anguish for the molested child.

FIRST RESPONSE

When you, as counselor, begin dealing with a child or teenage abuse victim, there are several things to address. Your first priority must be to ensure that the young person is safe from any further abuse. Research studies have concluded that approximately 60% of children are re-abused and subsequent incidents are even more serious.

Typically, when cases are reported, the sexual offender is ordered to leave the home and is not allowed to have unsupervised visits with the child. However, there are instances where the children are forced to leave the home, rather than the offender, causing them to feel as though *they* are the ones being punished. When this happens, it's important to communicate to them exactly what is going on and why. It can be very overwhelming for any child to be suddenly taken away from everything he's known and then thrust into an unfamiliar environment.

Once it has been determined that a child has been molested—especially in the case of penetration—he or she should receive a comprehensive physical examination immediately. You may cringe at the thought of the child being forced to endure such a thing, but it is absolutely necessary to have a medical doctor determine if there's been any physical damage so the victim can be promptly treated. If there is no injury, you can reassure the child that everything is alright physically.

In many instances, the courts become involved and the offender is sent to jail. When this happens, the youngster will need your emotional and spiritual support throughout the legal process. You can set the child's mind at ease—that he or she is now safe—without overstating it. One of the worst things that can happen to a child is to be led to believe that the abuser is gone forever, only to have him show up after a six-month stint in jail. While you understandably want to comfort and allay the victim's fears, be honest and explain this possibility to him or her. Help the child to understand that the arrest and the criminal proceedings that follow are a direct result of the offender's actions. Keep in mind that a child often feels enormous guilt for reporting the abuse, especially after the abuser is sent to jail.

Moreover, the child will probably be interviewed by social workers, child protection officials, attorneys and law enforcement officers and be required to describe repeatedly the abuse in detail to perfect strangers. The help of a loving counselor can be of invaluable support to the child through this entire ordeal.

Ongoing Counseling

Survival of the judicial process is only the beginning. As indicated in the examples above, there is much emotional damage done to the sexually abused victim that must be addressed. You must diligently seek to establish a rapport with the child whose trust and respect for adults has been shattered. While it is good for you to demonstrate love to the child (i.e. giving them a hug), you should always ask permission before touching the child in any way.

Along with instilling trust, you must also reestablish respect for authority. This requires patient, loving instruction. Avoid falling into humanistic pity which does nothing more than empower the child to use his or her newfound "victim" status for selfish purposes. The wise counselor gives love and encouragement but never allows a child to control the relationship or use it as a way to manipulate others.

As the proper relationship between you and the child is formed, you can now begin to address other deep-seated issues resulting from the abuse. Fear is perhaps the most common reaction exhibited by a child abuse victim. There is a place for proper fear and a healthy respect for danger. However, when a child becomes preoccupied with the idea that someone may harm him or her and protecting self becomes an obsession, it is displeasing to God. An effective biblical counselor will patiently show the child that preoccupation with oneself can be sinful and that it would be much better to focus one's thoughts upon pleasing God.

Another common emotional reaction manifested in abused children is anger, which ranges from seething bitterness, to depression, to rebellion, or even to explosive rage. The offender is typically the main object of the child's anger. However, it is not uncommon for the youngster to be angry with the mother for not doing more to protect him or her. Some even get mad at God for allowing the abuse to occur in the first place. It is extremely important that the child be taught to handle his or her feelings in a biblical way. (The story of how Joseph's brothers mistreated him and the way he responded is a wonderful illustration of the proper biblical response.) This helps the victim to see that, even though people may attempt to harm us, we have a sovereign God watching over everything that occurs in our lives, and He knows how to bring good out of the worst of situations.

You must instruct the child that it is wrong to repay evil for evil and that God expects Christians to overcome evil by doing good. (Romans 12:21) The importance of the New Testament concept of forgiveness must also be emphasized. True forgiveness occurs when the victim commits himself neither to dwell on the offense in his mind nor to bring it up again to the offender or others. This doesn't mean that the child can't work through the feelings of it in the positive setting of a counseling session or be honest in criminal proceedings. It simply means that they agree to do their best not to hold onto it as a means of vengeance.

Another feeling the child inevitably deals with is guilt. Some children feel as though they have betrayed a trust by disclosing what has happened to them. Others feel shame over what they have done, even though they did nothing to initiate it. This becomes especially true when they experience physical pleasure as their bodies respond the way in which God created them. However, even though the perpetrators are 100% at fault for everything that has occurred, young people sometimes do have things for which they are also legitimately at fault. As the counselor, it is important for you to understand that guilt is not primarily a feeling; it is culpability for a violation of God's Word. If, for instance, the victim is a young teenage girl and she eventually gets to the place where she begins craving the physical attention she has been receiving, experiencing a sense of guilt over her actions is right. Or, if the young person has developed hatred for the abuser, he or she must repent of this attitude and forgive him. As a biblical counselor you must help the young counselee distinguish between true and false guilt.

Clearly the victim of child abuse has many issues to work through. However, a loving, godly counselor can help to minimize the negative effects—such as depression, anxiety, paralyzing fear, paranoia, etc.—of the molestation and steer the victim away from a self-destructive path of habitual sin. What a joy it is for the counselor who comforts young victims and helps them respond in a way that pleases God![1]

COUNSELING TEENAGERS ABOUT MASTURBATION

Jeremy sat slouched in the chair across from me as he attempted to find the right words to describe his struggle. His sagging spirit and angry outbursts had created alarm with his parents, who insisted he meet with me (his pastor). A cloud of guilt and despair hovered in the atmosphere of my office. His eyes were cast to the floor, and his posture signaled that he'd long ago given up any hope of winning the battle.

After lovingly prodding and gently questioning him, I discovered that this young teenager was battling with masturbation. Feeling defeated, Jeremy began to doubt if there really was an all-powerful God who hears prayer. Where was God? Why was the temptation still so overwhelming? He'd begged God to deliver him from this temptation, but his repeated failures had left him frustrated and skeptical.

How would you counsel Jeremy? Would you laugh out loud and brush it off as nothing to be concerned about? Would you tell him to accept masturbation as God's gift to the single man? Absolutely not! A godly counselor would begin by telling Jeremy the truth. Although masturbation is not specifically mentioned, an honest study of Scripture reveals the wrongness of it. (See *Chapter Eleven, Answers to Five Moral Questions.*)

Jeremy needs to be told that although it is wrong, it is not an unpardonable sin! With his feet firmly planted on truth, one can now give him hope. He should be reminded that the fight against sin is one that every believer shares. He should also be assured that God has not abandoned him but has provided a "way out" (I Corinthians 10:13) that the two of you will seek together.

Having firmly established truth in his young mind, now it is time to give him some practical steps which will help him re-structure his life. You must help him to see that it will require more than a few minor alterations to cut something as powerful as lust and masturbation out of his life. It will require "radical amputation." (Matthew 5:29-30) Warn him that if he attempts to simply keep it at bay, then his efforts are doomed from the start. A few questions will help Jeremy think through what he can do to protect himself from temptation in the future: When is he usually tempted to masturbate? What are the events leading up to the temptation? Who are the people or places that stir the temptation most? He will probably need to "amputate" some people, places, idle time, and certain media intake from his life. Ask Jeremy to prayerfully consider this principle and then bring you a written list of the changes he needs to make in his life to break the habit of masturbation. You can assist in making it practical and attainable, and then hold him accountable to the new structure.

Another effective tool to use for Jeremy is a burning "Yes!". Too often our counsel to someone struggling in sin is littered with "No's" throughout, but we fail to give him anything new to replace the sin. The Bible doesn't just com-mand us to stop sinning but tells us to replace it with godli-ness. (II Timothy 2:22) It would be wise to give reading assign-ments (biblical and extra-biblical) that will stoke the flame in Jeremy's heart to know God in a greater way. Encourage him to establish and maintain a regular, vibrant devotional life. Help him to see the importance of meditating on some of the Psalms that extol the pleasures found in God. (Psalms 34, 36, 37, 42, 61, 62) Unless Jeremy begins to "taste and see that the Lord is good" (Psalm 34:8), he will keep returning to the same trough he's been eating from. Awaken his spiritual taste buds to the glory and wonder of knowing and reveling in God's presence. Then, hopefully, when that next temptation comes, he will stop and think, "Why would I sacrifice the satisfaction found in God for the cotton candy pleasures of the world?" As John Piper writes, "We must stock our minds with the superior promises and pleasures of Jesus."

Next, challenge Jeremy to start investing his life in other people. Nothing defeats a self-centered lifestyle like doing some good work that will benefit others. This kind of self-less service will destroy the tendency to isolate, will draw him closer to God, and will help him escape the prison of self. Help him to implement Romans 12:11: *"Do not be sloth-ful in zeal, be fervent in spirit, serving the Lord."*

Finally, you should be prepared for a path of progress that has high's and low's. Don't expect Jeremy to rocket right out of this habit after your first meeting. Remember, old habits die hard, and sin of any stripe won't go down without a fight! Be patient with him, but watch his attitude. Is he stubborn and rebellious, resisting all your counsel or dragging his heels? Is he weak and uninformed? Does he look like he's faint-hearted? Ask God to give you discernment about his heart. His condition doesn't change the truth or principles of God's Word, but it's certainly a factor as to how to apply that Word to his life. The Bible does not take a "one-size-fits-all" approach to the problems people face. As First Thessalonians 5:14 tells us, *"Now we exhort you, brethren, warn those who are unruly, comfort the faint-hearted, hold on to the weak, be patient with all."*

As soul physicians we must pray for discernment to apply the ointment of His Word to the right spot, in the right measure, and in the right way. We are exhorted to restore Jeremy and others *"in a spirit of gentleness, considering yourself lest you also be tempted."* (Galatians 6:1) If we wield the "double-edged sword" with gentleness and love, we can anticipate great success in our efforts to help teenagers overcome the habit of masturbation.[2]

eight

MINISTERING TO THE HURTING WIFE

Whathat can be more devastating for a wife than discovering her husband has a secret fascination with pornography and other women? Typically, wives who encounter this dilemma face a host of different emotions, feelings and situations.

One of the first reactions a wife experiences when discovering her husband's secret sin is a sense of betrayal. My wife Kathy beautifully articulates what so many women have experienced: *

> To me our intimacy was sacred. Saying "I do" at the altar made it exclusive and therefore off-limits to others. He was mine and I was his. What we had together in private was ours, and I was the only one who should know him in that way. Marital sex is the tie that physically binds two individuals together and its sanctity is due to the spiritual union that is created.

---

* In this chapter, I will quote liberally from my wife's book.

When I found out that Steve was being unfaithful, I was crushed. He was spiritually becoming "one flesh" with anything with a skirt, giving away what was MINE! Our circle of unity had been broken—our marriage bed defiled. We no longer had that special oneness which belonged only to us. Our sexual intimacy had been cheapened—actually nullified—because it was shared with many others. It had little or no value to him because he preferred a cheap thrill rather than the real thing: me, his wife. The pleasure he wanted from our union could be found or purchased on any street corner or in any massage parlor.

As far as I was concerned there was now nothing left that was ours as a married couple. We were just two people living together, sharing space. It killed me. Day after day the pain of the reality that our marriage was gone swept over me like sea billows.[1]

Another emotion that wells up within a jilted wife's heart is anger (perhaps even leading to unforgiveness). It is predictable that a woman suffering through the sense of betrayal described above should become very angry. She has given her heart to her husband and joined her life with his. In turn, he has treated her commitment with disdain. The deeper the love a person has for someone, the more intense the pain when that love is spurned. Anger is the natural reaction to such betrayal.

The wife who has been hurt this deeply no doubt becomes very suspicious of her husband. This can, to some degree, be a healthy response. Especially since, as long as she remains oblivious to her husband's sneaky ways, he can keep his sin continually hidden. Unfortunately, suspicions can also become a source of torment, often leading wives to imagine the worst. Left to her own natural thoughts, she can easily conjure up all kinds of scenarios. The enemy often exacerbates the situation further by feeding those inner fears. The devil loves to torment the hurting wife with mental pictures of her husband sleeping with every woman he encounters.

These are but a few of the many conflicting emotions plaguing this brokenhearted wife. Add to them all the other issues surrounding sexual sin (the need to be the spiritual leader in the home, accountability and added precautions for him, the involvement of other people in the situation, etc.) and one can readily sympathize with her feeling absolutely overwhelmed by her husband's habitual sexual sin.

At the risk of oversimplification, our examination of this complex subject is divided into two categories: 1) helping the woman whose husband is sincerely trying to overcome his problems, and 2) helping the wife of an unrepentant sinner. Many of the issues confronting these two groups differ both in severity and solution.

HELPING THE WIFE OF A SINCERE SINNER

I don't mean to minimize the suffering a woman goes through when discovering her husband's sin. However, the woman who is married to a man who honestly desires freedom has a much easier path before her.

When in his right mind, her husband wants to be faithful. This is evidenced by the numerous steps he has taken to overcome his habitual sin: He maintains a daily devotional life. He holds himself accountable to a spiritual mentor. He fights the urge to give in to temptation—increasingly winning more battles. In short, he is headed in the right direction.

The main responsibility of this man's wife is helping him through the grueling process of finding victory. Elsewhere I wrote:

Any wife who is going to help her husband through the process of overcoming this habit will have to closely monitor a number of things, the first being his money. As soon as I was serious about obtaining the victory over sexual sin, my wife and I agreed that I was not to have more than five dollars in my pocket at a time. I was not allowed to have a credit card or an ATM card. This one safety valve was an extremely important part of the victory which ensued. The man who means business will not hedge on this issue. Secondly, she must be attuned to her husband's problem and keep a close watch over his actions. If he suddenly stands up and announces that he needs to go shopping, she should question him about his exact intentions. The wife who is deceived a few times quickly learns to become suspicious about any odd behavior. Once again, a man who wants to be set free will appreciate and welcome such devotion from his spouse.

Naturally, one of the areas that may be out of her reach is his job. However, if he works at a factory, office, or store, and simply cannot leave his job, she can rest assured that he is less likely to get into trouble while at work. She will know exactly what time to expect him home from work every night. If he says that he has to work overtime, she will dutifully examine his pay check.[2]

As her counselor, your job is to coach her through

this important role in her husband's restoration. Her support through this journey could very well mean all the difference in his level of commitment. You must encourage her to encourage him! A wife who exhorts her husband in this battle against besetting sin is an incredible source of inspiration to the sincerely repentant man. To such a wife, Kathy wrote:

> I appreciate so much your sincere desire to be a blessing to your husband. Life's a lot easier when you have a husband who is really trying to do what's right. The key to his living victoriously is faithfulness and endurance. If he remains diligent and chooses to do those things God has shown him, he will make it!
>
> Your role is to be his cheerleader, not just when he scores a touchdown, but even after he fumbles the ball! Don't ever hold his mistakes against him. As best as you can, create an atmosphere of grace for him. Let him know that you are totally committed to him. No matter what kind of day he's had, show him that you are in his corner. His sincere desire to walk in victory will enable you to be completely supportive.[3]

Helping the Wife of an Unrepentant Sinner

The wife of a man who stubbornly wants his sin has a much greater challenge before her. In this case, you need to be her spiritual advisor, comforting friend and emotional cheerleader! She must traverse rough waters, requiring much godly wisdom. In this section, I briefly touch on some of the more urgent issues you should address with her.

First, if he is a believer, she should confront his sin.* We have already discussed the process of church discipline. If, after repeatedly questioning him about his sin, he is still unresponsive or evasive, she must involve the pastor:

> I suggest that you make an appointment with your pastor. Explain to him your situation and ask him to speak with your husband...
>
> More than likely your husband will become angry and see this as an invasion of privacy. No doubt such exposure will be humiliating to him. At any rate, it is important for you to be strong and compassionate through the whole ordeal. As you prepare to do this, you will face a strong temptation to call the whole thing off. Resist it! You will do him a tremendous disservice if you continue to ignore his hypocrisy. If his wife won't love him enough to confront him, who will?
>
> Don't feel guilty for bringing others into this. It would be unmerciful on your part if you cover up for him and pretend that everything is fine. Again, he may get upset with you, but that's all right. [4]

When counseling couples in these difficult situations, occasions do arise wherein a separation becomes necessary. Consider the case of the wife whose husband uses an explosive temper to manipulate and control her. Kathy gives her some practical advice:

---

* There is no scriptural support for confronting the sin of an unbeliever. It may very well be necessary, but the specific aim is different from that of confronting a believing husband. If for no other reason than making him aware, the wife of an unbelieving husband should share with him how his actions are affecting her.

You must first take control of the situation. *You* are allowing your husband to control you with his anger. This keeps you beaten down and unable to find God for yourself. It also keeps him from seeing his desperate need for God.

I believe your circumstances are severe enough to warrant an immediate separation from him as well as a restraining order. If you are fearful of him because of his violent, controlling nature, I suggest that you take the kids and leave when he's at work. (You might check with an attorney before pursuing this course of action.)

Once you've left, be aware of the fact that you will naturally start to crave his affection and attention again. You will probably second-guess your decision to leave. An overwhelming sense of insecurity may rise up within you. This may prompt you to remember his positive side or even reminisce about your happiest moments with him. Meanwhile, your memory of his abusiveness will fade. If you feel an overwhelming temptation to contact him "just to see how he's doing," resist it! Don't be caught off guard! The less contact the better.

Give him a few days to simmer down and allow reality to settle in. When you speak to him, be calm and aloof. Don't talk to him if he is in a rage, and don't let him sweet-talk you into coming home right away. Remember: he's a controller and will use every angle possible in order to get his own way. Just cut him off and keep the conversation strictly business (i.e. controlled visits with the kids, bills, and etc.). Once you have left, you will have control of the situation. Don't give it up!

In time, if he truly repents and turns to the Lord, his frantic efforts to get you back will be replaced with a new passion for Jesus. This is what you're looking for: "fruits of repentance." [5]

I share this situation because it describes some of the practical realities encountered in a marital separation. Whether or not the husband has an anger problem, sometimes a separation is the best course of action when sexual sin is involved.

My own story is a perfect example of the effective use of a separation. In 1982, Kathy and I were living in Los Angeles. By this point, my sin had degenerated into the most abominable behavior. Kathy finally snapped and left me, moving back to Sacramento. At first, I saw this as an opportunity to pursue my sin with greater abandon. Unbeknownst to me, God was giving me over to "impurity." After three weeks, my life unraveling around me, I finally humbled myself to God and surrendered my heart to Him. Had Kathy stayed with me, however, I don't know that I would have ever repented. Her leaving me was the jolting wake-up call I needed.

Some men in habitual sexual sin are, as I certainly was, in flagrant and open rebellion against God. They make no pretense about their sinful lifestyles. Their hardheartedness, while distressing, does at least bring clarity to the situation for the wife. However, other men, though seemingly sincere in seeking freedom, have a concealed, not-so-obvious spirit of rebellion. Kathy describes one such situation in her book:

> Unfortunately, many of those in sexual sin never experience true repentance. Although they may cry over their sin, plead with God to set them free, and make determined "efforts" at achieving victory or solemn vows to never go back, they haven't truly had an inward change of heart.
>
> I remember a couple named Bill and Fran we counseled some time ago. They had been married

eight years and had two small children by the time Bill entered our live-in program. He had a track record of unfaithfulness. Like so many men in sexual sin he would seemingly do good for some time but would then go on another binge of sexual sin. Each time the tears of sorrow and promises of "I'll never do it again!" would stream forth. "I don't know why God won't set me free!" Bill would protest. "I'm doing everything I know to do to get victory," he would exclaim with a tinge of resentment toward the Lord. Fran even found herself getting angry with God because she was so convinced that her husband had sincerely repented.

During this whole period Bill had led Fran to believe that his problems were limited to pornography. However, he had been unfaithful to her, visiting prostitutes. It was only by chance—divine chance, that is—that she found out about Pure Life Ministries at the same time she discovered all of this...

For several weeks, Bill did everything right in the live-in program. He did his homework—earnestly. He did what his counselors told him to do. He listened attentively to the messages preached in our chapel services. He continually expressed a desire to mature as a Christian, but still, he had not experienced any real breakthroughs. Was there a lack of motivation? Was he still clinging to some secret sin? Did he have a hidden agenda? Only time would tell.

Before long, we began suspecting that Bill's tearful bouts of repentance were insincere. Then one day we found out that he had been coming on to some woman at his job. It became clear to us all that, despite all of his protests to the contrary, he simply wasn't truly repenting of his sin. He had been willing to obey God only to a certain extent but balked when God started asking for a full surrender...

Bill's insincerity became obvious after Fran served him his divorce papers and he quit the live-in program. There was no longer a reason to continue the charade.

Repentance often comes in stages. A man who has been deeply entrenched in sexual sin will have years of ingrained habits to contend with. He will struggle with feelings of hopelessness, which paralyze even the most well-intentioned. All of this is in addition to the great love he has had with his sin. But, nevertheless, if he is sincere, changes will begin to occur as he is given new direction and real hope through Jesus Christ.[6]

THE GOAL OF THE COUNSEL

As a biblical counselor, you are entrusted with giving the wife godly wisdom and sympathetic encouragement. You must be an objective third party who can help her work through the complex issues that surface. Indeed, everything discussed thus far has revolved around such practical matters. However, please remember that the same overriding goal of counseling a sexual sinner should also drive one's efforts with the wife: "...we proclaim Him, admonishing every man and teaching every man with all wisdom that we may present every man complete in Christ." (Colossians 1:27b-28)

The inevitable temptation that arises, when counseling a devastated and despondent woman, is to afford human pity the foundational role in your efforts to help her. Of course, sympathy toward her victimization is a legitimate feeling, but a counseling structure built upon human sympathy alone is likely to do more harm than good. Self-pity, fostered sometimes by an overly-sympathetic approach, is an extremely powerful emotion that should be avoided at all cost. If allowed to fester, it creates a deadly environment that harbors and justifies bitterness, unforgiveness and even hatred.

Godly compassion, by contrast, offers sincere concern and an understanding ear, without fostering anything that could take her away from God. It is right to "weep with those who weep," but the woman's spiritual well-being must be the preeminent issue in the counselor's mind. What does God want to accomplish in her life through these circumstances? How can I help her gain the most spiritual and eternal benefit from this situation? These are the issues that are of paramount importance.

As you face these heart-wrenching situations, you must always provide a godly perspective, a compassionate heart and wise counsel.

nine

HELPING THE HOMOSEXUAL

There is currently a fierce debate between homosexual activists and leaders of the ex-gay movement. The dispute is over the origins of homosexual desire. The homosexual community staunchly contends that God created them with same-sex attractions, and therefore their behavior cannot be considered sinful. They avow that they were born with a genetic or biological predisposition toward homosexuality and cite several scientific studies to support their claims.* On the other hand, those in the ex-gay movement point out that all of these studies have glaring weaknesses and smack of partisanship. Dr. James Dobson points out:

I am certain that homosexuality does not result from irresistible genetic influences, as some

---

* Simon Levay of the Salk Institute in San Diego; Michael Bailey of Northwestern University and Richard Pillard of the Boston University School of Medicine; Dean Hamer of the National Cancer Institute; etc.

would have us believe. First, if it were specifically a genetic trait, then all identical twins would either have it or not have it. Their genes are exact duplicates, so anything deriving specifically from their DNA would express itself identically in the two individuals. Such is not the case. There are thousands of identical twins with whom one is gay and the other is straight.

Second, inherited characteristics that are not passed on to the next generation are eliminated from the gene pool. Since homosexuals and lesbians reproduce less frequently than heterosexuals, there should be a steadily decreasing number of people in the population with homosexual tendencies—especially over the many thousands of years mankind has been on the earth. There is, however, no indication that its numbers are in decline.

Third, and related to the same point, Scripture refers to epidemics of homosexuality and lesbianism that occurred in specific cultures...

Again, if homosexuality were inherited within the human family, it would be constant over time and within cultures. There would not be surges and epidemics as the apostle Paul referred to and as we appear to be seeing today. [1]

The truth is that homosexual desire does not appear to originate from any single source. Rather, it seems far more likely that such desires develop in different people in a variety of ways. It should be added here that none of the following scenarios, in and of themselves, dictate that homosexual desires are inevitable, but they *may* provide the opportunity for them to develop in some individuals.

FAMILY DYNAMICS

The stereotypical male homosexual grows up with a strong mother and a weak or absent father. The absence of a solid male role model seems to create a certain need inside some little boys during their formative years, which may lead them to seek acceptance through sexual activity later on in life. Although it may begin in a misguided attempt to gain approval and/or attention from other males, it quickly becomes intertwined with the adolescent's budding sex drive. At some point during puberty, the two cravings can become fused into an integrated inner compulsion. The more this burgeoning homosexual lust is entertained and acted upon, the more it becomes ingrained in the young man's psyche. These thought patterns become even more deeply entrenched as he surrounds himself with other homosexuals.

Take Gene for example. The oldest of four children, he always longed to be close with his father and often wondered why *his* dad wasn't warm, caring, and involved in his life like the fathers of other children. Gene's father rarely spent any time with the family—always too busy working, drinking, or having affairs with other women. So this meant that his mother had the dual task of disciplinarian and caregiver. A deep resentment began to develop in the young boy's heart toward his father.

Gene does not recall ever having a sexual attraction to men as a young boy. In fact, he looked forward to the day he could win some young girl's heart. At age 10, he and one of his male cousins began to experiment sexually with each other. While many other boys do the same and go on to live heterosexual lives, Gene had discovered a way to gain "acceptance" from men and satisfy his desire to have sex. In his case, the lack of a loving father seems to have made him more vulnerable to the enticements of homosexuality.

At first, these desires lay dormant within him, but as he entered into his teen years, his attraction toward men grew. Although he was sexually active with several girls during this time, just after he turned 20, he had his first homosexual encounter as an adult. This experience set him on a downward spiral of degradation that would last for almost ten years. Eventually he found victory at Pure Life.

MOLESTATION

Others are exposed to homosexuality as a result of being molested as children. Such experiences can ignite homosexual lust, which is further inflamed by pornography, fantasy, and other similar encounters as they grow older.

When he was nine years old, Matt was molested by his friend's older brother. After that experience, he initiated homosexual encounters with other boys his age. He continued this habit throughout his teenage years and on into adulthood.

Matt also cannot remember ever having any attraction toward men before his first experience, but the difference between him and Gene was that his family dynamics definitely did not fit the stereotype mentioned previously. Unquestionably, his problems began the day he was molested.

Julie was terribly abused as a young girl. Her father was an alcoholic who repeatedly molested her. To make matters even worse, he also made her have sex with his friends. She never had the kind of love and emotional nurturing that all children need. As a young teenager, she dealt with the pain by becoming promiscuous. She went through a number of sexual relationships with teenage boys. As she got older, she came to hate feeling used by males and sought comfort and security in other women through lesbian relationships.

PORNOGRAPHY INFLUENCE

Jerry's entrance into the realm of homosexuality was completely unforeseen. Even though he was a sexual addict, he was unquestionably the macho type—a "man's man." The thought of any sexual involvement with another man had always been repulsive to him. However, as his addiction to pornography and illicit sex grew, he found that the level of gratification he received from it began to diminish. As he continued to spiral downward, his craving for sex launched his curiosity for more degrading behavior.

Because he spent years watching couples have sex in pornographic videos, he became fascinated with the male anatomy. He began having "bisexual" experiences in the movie arcades of adult bookstores. At first he only allowed homosexuals to gratify him. But, once he crossed *that* line, he became susceptible to further temptation. While his sexual encounters with women became less satisfying, his interest in men continued to grow. One day he finally gave over to his new lust. Before long, *he* became the aggressor in the bookstores looking for other men. His obsession with homosexuality became so powerful that he gave up heterosexual experiences altogether.

CULTURAL INFLUENCE

Historically, homosexuality has always flourished in prosperous, licentious cultures. Over the past 40 years the "gay" lifestyle has spread like wildfire in America.

Are the staggering statistics of homosexuality a true indication of how many people are born that way—as the homosexual activists would have us believe—or is it simply that in today's permissive society, many choose a lifestyle of perversion simply because it's so readily accessible? I believe the latter to be true.

Sam's story is a good illustration of this. Although he was always a sensitive young boy, he never had any homosexual desires until some of his friends took him to a gay nightclub one night. Because he had always been a loner, this was the first time he had ever really felt accepted by others. The excitement of that experience coupled with the availability of easy sex catapulted him into the gay lifestyle which he openly embraced for many years. Eventually, he became a Christian and fought his way out of his addictive behavior.

The Depravity of Man

There is one more avenue into homosexuality that cannot be ruled out. I am referring to those individuals who seem to have an inherent attraction toward their own gender that cannot be explained in any of the aforementioned scenarios.

Dr. James Dobson is one of the few Christian activists—if not the only one—who will not absolutely discard the concept that some people seem to be born with same-sex desires:

> No one can say definitively what causes a person to be homosexual. We have to acknowledge that there could be inheritable tendencies (which does not make homosexuality "involuntary") in some individuals. There is no proof of such influence to this point, but we can't rule it out in specific cases. It could also result from the presence or absence of hormonal "spiking" that typically occurs before birth... While homosexuality and lesbianism are not exclusively in-

duced by heredity, it is important to emphasize that it often occurs in those who did not choose it. Some individuals are drawn toward the gay lifestyle in the absence of any known related influences.[2]

Personally, I do not have a problem with the idea that some individuals may have inherent homosexual desires. There is an element here that must be touched upon in this discussion. The notion of such a genetic predisposition is in the realm of possibility simply because mankind has a fallen nature that is bent towards evil. The Word of God clearly states that sin entered the human race at the Fall in the Garden. That single event corrupted the physiological, psychological, and spiritual makeup of mankind in ways that we don't fully understand. (Genesis 3)

Consequently, living in a sin-cursed world with a fallen nature predisposes all of us to different types of temptation. There's not a person alive who doesn't have to overcome some inherent attraction to sin. The fact that some individuals have a propensity toward homosexual lust shouldn't surprise us. Homosexual lust is a result—either directly or indirectly—of the Fall.

HANDLING OBJECTIONS

Occasionally the counselor will find himself in a situation where he must help a homosexual who has been influenced by the gay activists' viewpoint. That individual needs someone to help him see the deception involved. The following are some of the arguments one might encounter from such a person:

Objection 1: *"I was born this way."*

When an individual makes this claim, he is often simply

excusing his behavior as if God has condoned it. For example, it might be true that from his earliest days he has had certain "softer" tendencies (e.g. interested in the arts rather than football) and has therefore been susceptible to homosexual temptation, but that does not justify behavior that is clearly unscriptural and ungodly.*

Regardless of what causes homosexual lust to develop, a person still has a *choice* as to whether he will give himself over to it or not. As I have stated earlier, every one of us is predisposed toward some sin. James said, "But each one is tempted when he is carried away and enticed by his *own* lust." (James 1:14) There are a myriad of sins and countless different lusts to provoke them. Sexual lust is only one of many. Consequently, the *origin* of the homosexual desire isn't the key issue. People who have a bent toward homosexuality must resist those desires of the flesh, repent of their sin, and commit themselves to living in obedience to God's Word just as a person who struggles with any other life-dominating sin.

Objection 2: *"It is unfair for God to allow me to have homosexual tendencies and then to demand that I renounce them."*

In her book, *When His Secret Sin Breaks Your Heart*, my wife Kathy wrote the following in response to a letter she received from a woman married to a man who had given in to his homosexual fantasies:

> I understand your struggles with the unfairness of it all. "My husband didn't ask to have these feelings. It just doesn't seem fair!" Janice, is it fair that a little girl is born blind? Is it fair that a little boy is born addicted to crack? Is it fair that another is men-

---

* Leviticus 18:22; 20:13; Romans 1:26-27; 1 Corinthians 6:9-10.

tally retarded? I could go on and on, of course. The human race has been messed up ever since the fall of our first parents in the Garden. Furthermore, we have to remember that since then this world has been controlled by a very evil presence—the devil and his angels. He is called a murderer and destroyer for good reason.

But glory to God! We have a faithful, loving Father who is ever ready to lead us into the abundant Christian life if we will only turn to Him with all of our hearts. There is no reason for anybody to live out his life on this earth in misery, no matter how bad his circumstances or struggles are.

You must realize that your husband has never truly yielded his heart to God. He has gone through the motions of Christianity, but hasn't given his all to the Lord. Therefore, he has been unable to appropriate all that God had for his life. His lack of real commitment has resulted in a lack of real victory. Finally, in self-pity, he has thrown in the towel to pursue and fulfill his lustful desires, having convinced himself that he had given God every opportunity to set him free.

Pray that he will soon come to see the emptiness of the homosexual lifestyle and then will repent and seek God with all of his heart.[3]

Objection 3: *"You don't understand!"*

"Yes, it's true," you might respond. "I don't know what it's like to have to deal with homosexual desires and all that goes with it. However, I do have first-hand experience in the struggle against overwhelming desires to sin. I do understand what it's like to deny those desires. I do know what it means to turn to God in the midst of those powerful temptations."

The Christian counselor has his own testimony of how God has helped him to overcome the hold of sin and mature in the faith. Though people may debate about teachings and biblical interpretations, they cannot argue with a believer's personal testimony. That is why the apostle Paul constantly shared his own story when he preached to others. (cf. Acts 9, etc.)

Perhaps even more important is the spiritual truth referred to in Scripture: "For we do not have a high priest who cannot sympathize with our weaknesses, but One who has been tempted in all things as we are, yet without sin." (Hebrews 4:15) This is why Jesus "...is able to come to the aid of those who are tempted." (Hebrews 2:18) And why Paul could so confidently state: "No temptation has overtaken you but such as is common to man; and God is faithful, who will not allow you to be tempted beyond what you are able, but with the temptation will provide the way of escape also, so that you will be able to endure it." (I Corinthians 10:13) There is a way of escape from the clutches of homosexual sin for those who truly want it.

Objection 4: *"The Bible says that David and Jonathan were lovers."*

This idea, and many others like it, have been concocted by gay rights activists from the following verse: "Now it came about when he had finished speaking to Saul, that the soul of Jonathan was knit to the soul of David, and Jonathan loved him as himself." (1 Samuel 18:1)

Yes, it is true that the Bible says that Jonathan and David had a great love for each other, but nowhere does it state or imply that their bond of love was homosexual in nature. Actually, they were simply obeying a commandment given to God's people hundreds of years prior to this. "You shall love your neighbor as yourself." (Leviticus 19:18b) Jesus showed the enormous importance of this commandment when He identified it as the second greatest commandment of all. (Matthew 22:38-40) To twist pure, selfless devotion to another person into something dirty and perverse shows how deceived many of these people are. (Titus 1:15) Actually, the Hebrew word for love found in this passage (*ahab*) is the same word used to describe Abraham's love for Isaac, which is hardly an example of homosexual lust.

Objection 5: *"If homosexuality is wrong, then why did I feel such a sense of relief when I 'came out of the closet?' Isn't that proof that I am doing the right thing; that I am being true to myself?"*

There is no question that homosexuals can experience relief or even exhilaration when they openly declare the lifestyle they have kept hidden for years. However, such elation and freedom of expression is only temporary and is a way to justify their sinful behavior.

I experienced this same feeling in 1983 when I left Bible school. I was growing weary of the restrictions that were placed on my life. Secret sin was eating away at my commitment to the Lord. I finally decided I had had enough. When I left school, I felt like 1,000 pounds had been lifted off my back. I felt so free! However, the truth was that I had simply traded one form of bondage for another. I exchanged God's merciful and loving boundaries for the terrible bondage of sin. I plummeted into nine more months of darkness before finally making a U-turn and battling my way back out. Was I in high spirits when I left school? The answer is yes, but that exuberance did not endorse or justify my actions.

Scripture teaches that it is dangerous to make life choices based upon emotions. Solomon wisely admonished his readers: "Trust in the LORD with all your heart and do not lean on your own understanding." (Proverbs 3:5) He later wrote, "There is a way which seems right to a man, but its end is the way of death." (Proverbs 14:12) Jeremiah also pointed out, "The heart is more deceitful than all else and is desperately sick; who can understand it?" (Jeremiah 17:9) Our Creator knows far better than we what is best for our lives.

Objection 6: *"Since my homosexual desires came about as a result of poor emotional nurturing in my childhood, the key to my recovery is to first heal my damaged emotions."*

This line of reasoning is rooted in a psychotherapeutic worldview and is widely embraced in the ex-gay community. While ex-gay leaders—in their debates with homosexual activists—contend that homosexual practices are sinful, their actual treatment of homosexuality actually minimizes its sinfulness. By strongly emphasizing the real or perceived emotional damage homosexuals may have experienced during childhood, they reduce the individual's culpability for his actions. Every conceivable factor that may have been involved with the formation of same-sex attractions is scrutinized and contemplated. The more these issues are examined, the more their importance becomes inflated. As the emotional pain an individual has suffered is increasingly magnified, the sense of his guilt diminishes. This line of thought takes the person from the position of being a sinner in need of repentance to a victim in need of emotional recovery.

There are a number of reasons why I do not agree with this line of reasoning. First of all, while homosexuality does carry its own unique problems (not the least of which is a social stigma attached to it), it is still just another form of sin and must be treated as such. Nowhere in Scripture are homosexuals presented as special cases who are exempt from the laws of the Kingdom of God. In fact, the Bible calls homosexuality "an abomination." (Leviticus 18:22) This abhorrence of homosexual practices continues into the New Testament. (Romans 1; I Corinthians 6; etc.) Homosexuals are responsible for their actions and should be treated with the same compassion and loving correction as anyone else involved in sinful behavior.

Secondly, it must be understood that attempting to gain acceptance from other males through sexual and/or emotional bonding is a sinful response to emotional pain. Of course, it is understood that adolescents who have experienced rejection and/or emotional abuse usually respond in unhealthy ways. However, this does not change the fact that every individual will be accountable before God for his behavior. A troubled childhood and difficult circumstances growing up do not justify sin. A godly counselor can help a hurting child (or adult) learn to make proper responses to painful experiences.

Thirdly, Scripture does not even remotely suggest that the solution to sin of any kind is to be found in "healing damaged emotions." Instead, the Bible uses stories, prayers, commandments and teachings to convey the fact that repentance is God's solution to sin. However, repentance only comes about as a person takes full responsibility for his actions—even to the point of sorrowing over them.* The person who continually excuses and minimizes his past sinful behavior, and attempts to lay the blame on others or on outside environmental influences will never experience the kind of brokenness that truly releases a person from the clutches of sin. His refusal to take responsibility for his actions is the very thing that keeps him from the liberating power of repentance.

---

* This experience of brokenness and repentance is systematically examined in *At the Altar of Sexual Idolatry.*

Lastly, emotional well-being comes when one changes the focus of his life from pleasing SELF to pleasing God. The fulfillment that comes through obedience and intimacy with the Lord brings all the healing an emotionally damaged person will ever need. Peter said, "Repent therefore and return, that your sins may be wiped away, in order that times of refreshing may come from the presence of the Lord." (Acts 3:19) Narcissism—extreme self-preoccupation—does not bring joy or emotional fulfillment. Rather, the more a person focuses on himself, the more miserable he becomes. Concentrating on knowing God in a very real way is the only path into "the joy of the Lord."

Objection 7: *"I've prayed, gone to church, read my Bible, repented and tried to change but my homosexual desires haven't gone away. What you teach simply doesn't work.*

Anyone who claims to have followed the principles outlined in Scripture to no avail is either sincerely mistaken or self-deceived. Typically, people who make these statements honestly believe they have tried to do things God's way. However, the truth is that their efforts have been very weak and miniscule.

Most people with a long history of habitual sin do not understand what a real devotional life is like. Perhaps they have sought the Lord, but those attempts have usually been inconsistent or of short duration. Any counselee who sincerely desires to overcome his addictive behavior must establish a solid and vibrant devotional life which requires a strong commitment and a great deal of effort. He must really put his heart into prayer and Bible study before there will be a noticeable change in life. If he remains faithful to it, eventually he will begin to see the power of God at work in his life. But this doesn't happen right away, and many give up without really allowing the Lord time to work in their lives. Those who claim to have repented and yet remain in habitual sin are clearly very confused. Repentance means the person has quit his sinful behavior. I wrote the following in *At the Altar of Sexual Idolatry*:

As the addict enters the beginning stage of remorse, he will often make certain promises to God vowing never to repeat the same sin again: "Lord, I swear I won't do this ever again!" As his eyes are opened to the reality of the horrible emptiness and nature of his sin, he readily makes such a vow; for, it is at this moment that he truly sees sin for what it really is.

However, the problem with making such a resolution is that it stems from the man's own strength and determination to resist and overcome an evil. This sort of "promise-keeping" will never endure future temptations in the same area. It is for this exact reason that the sex addict has attempted countless times before to break the habit, yet to no avail.

The man desperately needs repentance. True repentance comes when a man's heart has changed its outlook on sin. A man will only quit his sinful, destructive behavior when he has truly repented of it in his heart. As he moves closer to the heart of God, he begins to develop a "godly sorrow" over his sin.[4]

There is one other issue that should be addressed here as well: the ongoing presence of homosexual lust. Although his emotions are inextricably tied into his desires, it must be understood that, at its core, the desire for homosexual activity is simply a lust of the flesh. The lust for homosexual activity will only be as strong as the person is unbroken and living "in the flesh." As the believer begins to experience a genuine sorrow over his sin, experiences true repentance, and develops a strong devotional life, he will find that the temptation to engage in lascivious acts will gradually lose its power. Paul described this battle in Galatians 5: "But I say, walk by the Spirit, and you will not carry out the desire of the flesh. For the flesh sets its desire against the Spirit, and the Spirit against the flesh; for these are in opposition to one another, so that you may not do the things that you please... Now the deeds of the flesh are evident, which are: immorality, impurity, sensuality..." (Galatians 5:16-19)

It is wrong to expect these desires to quickly go away. Instead, the struggling believer must come to understand that those desires come from his fallen nature and the only way to live above them is through a repentant and Spirit-led life.

The immature believer may sincerely believe that he has tried the biblically-based method of overcoming habitual sin. However, the bottom line is if there has been genuine repentance, there will be noticeable fruit in his life. To suggest otherwise is to make God a liar.

Objection 8: *The thought of having sex with someone of the opposite sex is revolting to me."*

Homosexual sex is a form of perversion that can become ingrained in a person's mind. Earlier, I stated the following: "The more this burgeoning homosexual lust is entertained and acted upon, the deeper it takes hold in the young man's psyche. These thought patterns become even more deeply entrenched as he surrounds himself with other homosexuals." It is natural for a homosexual to feel comfortable with that kind of lust because he has spent years reinforcing it. In fact, homosexual lust has become so embedded in his thinking that it seems quite unnatural—even repulsive—for him to think about having sex with a female.*

Undeniably, most homosexuals have approached sex through lust or a selfish and corrupted desire to receive acceptance. They have never known what it is like to experience sex the way God intended it. Their idea of the sexual act has always been rooted in selfish desire.

Nevertheless, the man who has repented and been deeply broken over his sin, and has subsequently entered into true intimacy with God, will have a different experience. If and when the Lord arranges for him to become married, he will find that the wedding night will not involve dirty sex but will be based upon the divine love of God. (Hebrews 13:4) Although the concept of "making love" has lost its original meaning, it actually describes the purpose sex was created: two people expressing their devotion, commitment and deepest feelings for each other in a physical act. This is completely different than the utter selfishness involved in the typical homosexual encounter.

Helping the homosexual may seem to be a daunting task to a counselor, but as he intercedes for those who come to him for counsel, he will find the Holy Spirit alongside of him throughout the entire process offering him direction and aid. No one's problems are too great for God to overcome!

---

* The same holds true of a lesbian, of course.

ten

ASSISTING THE STRUGGLING PASTOR

Over the past fifteen years, the Church in America has been rocked by numerous sex scandals, as great numbers within its leadership ranks have fallen prey to the temptress of sexual sin. Surely Solomon spoke the truth when he said, "For she hath cast down many wounded: yea, many strong men have been slain by her." (Proverbs 7:26 KJV)

In a misguided attempt to explain this recurring phenomenon, some have employed First Corinthians 10:12 (Let him who thinks he stands take heed lest he fall.) as support of their theory that it can happen to anybody. "After all, even David fell," goes the familiar justifying refrain. The real culprit, of course, is the devil who tempted the poor minister with such overwhelming enticements that he just couldn't help himself.

While it is true that the enemy is masterful at laying snares before believers, equally true is the fact that *God has empowered His people to overcome the allurements of sin.* The factors contributing to a minister's fall into illicit sexual activity are clearly identifiable when viewed through the lens of Scripture.

PAUL'S WARNING

A correct interpretation of Paul's admonition to "take heed" requires a proper understanding of the context behind his statement. The historical backdrop of the tenth chapter of First Corinthians is the story of the Israelites living in the wilderness:

> And do not be idolaters as some of them were; as it is written, "The people sat down to eat and drink, and stood up to play." Nor let us act immorally, as some of them did, and twenty-three thousand fell in one day. Nor let us try the Lord, as some of them did, and were destroyed by the serpents. Nor grumble, as some of them did, and were destroyed by the destroyer. (I Corinthians 10:7-10)

The central theme of this chapter is the importance of living in obedience to God. The Jewish people, in outright defiance of God, had given themselves over to Egyptian idolatry. Because they consistently refused to repent of their carnality and worldliness, they were judged severely by the Lord. Having established a correlation between the ungodliness of the Israelites and that of the Corinthians, Paul uttered his warning: "Therefore let him who thinks he stands take heed lest he fall." This powerful exhortation was addressed to those who by willful choice have filled their lives with idolatry and immorality. Of course, every human has a fallen nature that is susceptible to sin; however, none need yield to its enticements. Paul went on to say:

> No temptation has overtaken you but such as is common to man; and God is faithful, who will

not allow you to be tempted beyond what you are able, but with the temptation will provide the way of escape also, that you may be able to endure it. (I Corinthians 10:13)

Paul's point is precisely the opposite of those claiming that anyone can fall at anytime. Although it is right to pray for, believe the best about, encourage and support those who have committed immorality, their behavior must be condemned—not excused under the premise that it can happen to anybody. People don't just "fall" into sin, as if they were walking along a path in the dark and suddenly—through no fault of their own—fell into a hole. There is always a reason why sin occurs. *Ultimately, people are vulnerable to temptation when their daily lives are not aligned with God's Word.* David's life epitomizes the truth of this statement.

THE FALL OF DAVID

The "Sweet Psalmist" of Israel had a unique hunger for the Lord from the time he was a young boy tending sheep in the wilderness. His spiritual appetite intensified as he spent time with Samuel and deepened during his years as a fugitive, running for his life from Saul. Undoubtedly, David was hitting his spiritual peak when he became king at the age of 30. Yet, within 20 years, he had committed the unthinkable: he lured Bathsheba into adultery and ordered her husband killed. The sight of him leering at her from his rooftop, arranging for her to come to his chambers, seducing her and then having her husband killed must have been enough to make angels sit down and weep. What a tremendous blow this was to the Kingdom of God!

How could it happen? The same way it can—*and does—*

happen to 21st Century Christian leaders. There were clear warning signs long before David committed his wicked deeds— warning signs that we too would be wise to watch for.

DANGER, DANGER, DANGER!

By the time he reached his forties, David had experienced the depths of God, penned most of the Psalms and led Israel to great victories. All the while he was headed straight for disaster. He couldn't see it coming because he— like many natural leaders—had been blinded by a sense of invincibility. Some, who have lost sight of their need for God's daily grace, boast, "I will never fall!" However, the apostle Paul strictly warns, "Take heed."

In my 18 years of helping men find freedom from sexual sin, I have learned to watch for five "red flags" when counseling those in ministry: *prayerlessness, pressure, prosperity, pleasure and power.* For the sake of simplicity, I will call them "P" flags:

"P" Flag # 1: *Prayerlessness.* It seems that the dangers and spiritual hunger that had kept David pressed into the Lord in his younger years were gradually replaced by a sense of satisfaction and security. Though no outward lack of godliness was visible, we can easily suppose that his inward panting for God's abiding presence began to diminish. Consequently, over time he lost his intimate connection with God.

In my years of helping fallen pastors, I have never had to minister to a "Mary," but I have dealt with many "Marthas." In other words, those who stay at the feet of Christ are not nearly as susceptible to sexual temptation as those who do not. Paul said, "Walk by the Spirit, and you will not carry out the desire of the flesh." (Galatians 5:16) The sensuous and seductive atmospheres that the enemy creates are very intoxicating to those who allow the demands of ministry to crowd out their time with God.

Jesus helped Martha to see that, while her intentions were noble, her efforts were misplaced. He told her, "Martha, Martha, you are worried and bothered about so many things; but only a few things are necessary, really only one, for Mary has chosen the good part, which shall not be taken away from her." (Luke 10:41-42) Echoing this appeal, Corrie Ten Boom once warned, "Beware of the barrenness of a busy life."

"P" Flag # 2: *Pressure.* God used David's leadership to usher in the most prosperous and powerful period in the entire history of the nation of Israel. However, as his government and military grew, so did the degree of his responsibility. The crushing weight of high-intensity leadership tends to drain a person's spiritual vitality—often at a time when he needs it most!

Many Church leaders face the same kind of stress today, which brings with it the potential for disaster. Scripture offers the solution when it says to, "put on the Lord Jesus Christ, and make no provision for the flesh in regard to its lusts." (Romans 13:14) Those in top positions, burdened by countless concerns, desperately need the abiding presence of Christ.

How dangerous it is to seek relief from stress by turning to the world! Making provision for the flesh literally means to provide for its sustenance—to keep it alive and healthy. For example, this is what the believer who idly watches television does to himself—something many ministers do to relieve stress. However, we must admit that most TV programming nowadays is simply the enactment of all the deeds of the flesh and does far more to corrupt than to edify. What may begin as a means to relax, entertain or unwind almost inevitably leads to a quenching of God's Spirit and a downward spiral spiritually.

The Christian leader carrying the weight of ministry cannot afford to diminish his spiritual life. Anything that leads him to Jesus strengthens his faith; anything that leads him away from God depletes his spiritual storehouse. This leaves him at risk to the enemy's schemes.

"P" Flag # 3: *Prosperity.* The Lord undoubtedly noticed the great sacrifices David made for the Kingdom of God during his early years. When He confronted David through Nathan, God told him, "I gave you the house of Israel and Judah. And if all this had been too little, I would have given you even more." (II Samuel 12:8 NIV) For 20 years, David reaped the bounty of God's goodness to him. Unfortunately, that same prosperity led him down a long road of self-indulgence, eventually leaving him spiritually weak and vulnerable.

I doubt if anything brings more joy to the Father's heart than blessing those who have remained faithful to Him through years of hardship. Those who have risen to the higher echelons of Church leadership are often well compensated for their efforts monetarily. This is certainly appropriate, for as the Bible says, "The laborer is worthy of his wages." (I Timothy 5:18)

I believe the purpose behind this injunction is that the extra finances afforded to the minister free him from some of the lesser concerns of daily life so he might be able to give himself more thoroughly to God's work. However, the inevitable danger inherent in having wealth is that it tends to diminish a person's dependence upon God. Furthermore, an abundance of money provides greater opportunity and ability to indulge in immoral activity.

"P" Flag # 4: *Pleasure*. David's prosperity and prominence allowed him to lavish himself with pleasure. Little wonder then that he, spying Bathsheba, lacked the inner strength to withstand the temptation to possess her.

The gravity of this subject should sober any modern-day believer especially given Paul's warning that in the last days many would be "lovers of pleasure rather than lovers of God; holding to a form of godliness, although they have denied its power..." (II Timothy 3:4-5)

Pleasure, kept in the right perspective, does have its place in life. However, when gratification becomes an expected part of life, it not only corrodes one's spiritual life, but it eventually chokes out everything that is wholesome.

Pornography and illicit sexual activity are merely extreme forms of pleasure. Therefore, the person who becomes addicted to pleasure and entertainment is himself very vulnerable to sexual temptation. People who increasingly fill their lives with "innocuous" pleasures find the step required to cross over into sinful pleasures getting progressively smaller. The apostle Paul described them as being "enslaved to various lusts and pleasures." (Titus 3:3)

"P" Flag # 5: *Power*. The old adage is true: "Power corrupts and absolute power corrupts absolutely." David's life is proof that everyone is susceptible to the hideous yet subtle influences of pride. A person who is reveling in the limelight of fame or recognition can easily become inflated by feelings of self-importance. The slippery slope of self-exaltation often leads to a fall. (Proverbs 16:18)

Perhaps King David thought he deserved Bathsheba, that she was his just reward for having given so much to Israel. Herein lies the danger of prominence: even the minister who begins his work serving others can arrive at a place where he believes himself so important that they should now meet *his* needs. In other words, the man called to be a servant to others now sees himself as their master.

Alexander MacClaren once said, "The humble mind thinks not of its claims on others, but of its duties to them." One of the reasons a Christian leader falls into sexual sin is that he has lost his sense of public responsibility to live above reproach. Once this occurs, disaster is imminent.

The warning signs I have listed are not meant to be comprehensive. Rather, they are mentioned to support what was stated earlier: *the way a believer lives his daily life will determine how vulnerable he is to the allurements of sin.* A man who is living a consecrated life, walking humbly with God, with his priorities in order may very well face temptations to fall into sin. However, in the midst of that temptation, he finds the grace of God which empowers him "to deny ungodliness and worldly desires and to live sensibly, righteously and godly in the present age." (Titus 2:12)

THE PASTOR WHO HAS FALLEN

I have provided the above guidelines so the counselor can better understand the challenges and needs of pastors. The counselor who is in a position to help a pastor before he falls into sin can utilize these principles to gauge areas of vulnerability and assist him in shoring up those weak spots. But what can be done for the pastor who has already gotten himself ensnared by some form of immorality?

When it comes to spiritual matters, no pit is dug so deep that one cannot also climb out of it. The five "P-Flags" all indicate aspects of a minister's life that are potential pitfalls. Has the pastor's devotional life withered up? Then he must discipline himself to resurrect it. In his stress, has he turned to the world's entertainment for comfort? Then he must begin extricating himself from it. Has prosperity affected his sense of dependence upon God? Then he must repent of self-trust and make a conscious effort to turn to the Lord to meet his daily needs. Has pleasure taken the place of God's presence in his life? Then he must renounce it and begin seeking the Lord with all his heart. Has he become corrupted by prestige? Then he must humble himself to God and others. Only by shoring up the weak areas of his spiritual life can he hope to get back on track with the Lord.

Putting his spiritual house in order should certainly be his primary focus. However, if sexual sin is involved, he must face some practical issues as well. As with any sin, confession plays an important role in the process of restoration. The question is: To whom does he confess? Should he admit his wrongdoing to his board? Should he come clean before the entire congregation? Should he confess to his denominational superiors? Or, is it enough that he has told you, his counselor?

The answer to these questions depends upon the extent of what he has done. If he has viewed pornography once or twice on the Internet over the course of some period of time, then coming into the light with his counselor or another minister should be sufficient. The important thing is that he establishes safeguards in his life to make sure that it doesn't happen again. He should immediately put a content filter on his computer or, perhaps even better than this, subscribe to an online "buddy system" that holds him accountable for his Internet use.* He should also tell his wife what

---

* One such program is Covenant Eyes (www.covenanteyes.com). The way it works is as follows: Every web site he visits is recorded and the list is forwarded to his accountability partner monthly. Any questionable sites that have been entered will be highlighted and placed at the beginning of the list. This way he will know that his accountability partner will discover any indiscretions.

he has done so that she too can be involved in the account-ability process.

If the pastor has an on-going pornography habit, he should confess what he has done in its entirety to his immediate supervisor. He should not confess this sort of problem to his board* or the congregation. The reason I say this is that, once he has admitted a moral failure, he loses credibility with his people. Though he has a pornography habit, his ministry can still be salvaged through the oversight of a wise superior. As a result of overcoming his addiction and getting his spiritual life back on track, he can once again be a useful vessel to the Lord. However, if he is unwilling to let go of the pornography, his supervisor should then take appropriate measures to deal with the situation.

The severity of the minister's predicament greatly increases when sexual activity with another person is involved. (Inclusive in this are behaviors such as peeping in windows or exposing himself to others.) The first thing he should do is confess to his wife and his immediate superior and then resign his ministerial position. He should also confess his sin (in general terms) to the congregation either by meeting with the board or by writing an open letter to the congregation. This letter would be read in church (or in a membership meeting) by a board member. Generally speaking, I would advise against standing in the pulpit and admitting his moral failure. Emotions in these situations can often supersede sound judgment. Some parishioners might react angrily, while others, motivated

---

* I include board with the congregation because, from my experience, once a pastor has admitted this sort of thing to board members, it will only be a matter of time before the rumors spread throughout the entire church.

by feelings of pity, could rashly assure him that he need not resign.*

DEALING WITH THE AFTERMATH

Regrettably, ministers who fall into sexual sin are often personally devastated by the inevitable public disgrace. One prominent radio preacher, whose indiscretions were disclosed nationwide, shared the following with me: "There are simply no words to describe the pain and agony my wife and I went through during the weeks, months, and years that followed. Not only were we rejected by those we considered to be our friends, but both the elders and the entire staff of the church refused to have any contact with us whatsoever. Yes, indeed, my ministry was shattered as a result of my own foolishness."

This story perfectly illustrates the terrible price that sin can exact upon a person's life. However, the most difficult (and crucial) issue confronting the man in this situation is the spiritual barrenness that preceded his fall from grace. Its magnitude is evident in David's prayer of repentance:

> Purify me with hyssop, and I shall be clean; wash me, and I shall be whiter than snow. Make me to hear joy and gladness, let the bones which You have broken rejoice. Hide Your face from my sins and blot out all my iniquities. Create in me a clean heart, O God, and renew a steadfast spirit within me. Do not cast me away from Your presence and do not take Your Holy Spirit from me. Restore to me the

---

* Let there be no question about the fact that any minister who has fallen into fornication must completely remove himself from leadership.

joy of Your salvation and sustain me with a willing spirit. (Psalm 51:7-12)

Your task in working with the fallen Christian leader is to help him come into true repentance. David's prayer exemplifies the perfect balance between godly sorrow over what he had done and bright hope that his God would respond with compassion to his pleas. It is a prayer of faith.

Though scripturally untrue, it may seem to the fallen pastor that all is lost. In reality, God is waiting for him with open arms and a gracious, welcoming smile. Yes, he has lost his ministry, but if he truly repents, the Lord can once again allow the blessings to flow into his life. While he must endure some of the consequences of his actions, the Lord is faithful to see him through the entire process. One day, if he continues to stay pressed into God, he might even be restored to ministry.

eleven

ANSWERS TO
FIVE MORAL QUESTIONS

Over the years, as I have spoken to various groups of ministers and counselors, certain questions regarding sexuality have frequently surfaced. My authority to tackle these subjects extends no further than the sure foundation of Scripture. However, since none of these topics are specifically addressed in the Bible (hence the questions), my answers must rest entirely upon a combination of established biblical concepts and a rudimentary understanding of the human conscience.

A GOOD CONSCIENCE

The apostle Paul once claimed that his instruction was "...from a pure heart and a good conscience and a sincere faith." (I Timothy 1:5) It should be evident that his teaching must also be *received* in the same spirit in which it was given. However, people tend to believe what they want to believe, according to their own preconceived notions. A sincere Christian, however, makes allowances for this natural tendency and does his utmost to approach such moral questions honestly and objectively.

What is the human conscience? According to *Vine's Dictionary*, the Greek word for conscience (*suneidesis*) literally means to have "co-knowledge" of something resulting in one's "sense of guiltiness before God." Thus, humans were created with a unique and intrinsic faculty that gives them an almost "third-person" perspective on the rightness and wrongness of their actions. When a person does something sinful his conscience is pricked by a sense of guilt.

The conscience physiologically is comparable to the human nervous system. When a man is physically wounded, a sense of pain races through his nervous system. This is the body's way of alerting him that something is wrong. Likewise, when a person sins, the human soul has a warning system that sounds an alarm alerting him to the fact that his actions have *wounded him spiritually*. The alarm of his conscience trumpets: "Mayday! Mayday! Something is wrong!" God has equipped every human being with this spiritual mechanism.

While the Bible clearly addresses the distinction between good and evil in relation to many behaviors, it was not written as a comprehensive treatment of every possible human action. Rather, the Scriptures lay down spiritual principles whereby a believer may properly govern his life. With the indwelling Spirit as a guide, the Christian perceives whether or not a certain type of behavior is morally acceptable to the Lord. Just as some people are more sensitive to pain than others, so too the saint who is "walking in the Spirit" tends to be much more aware of the Spirit's promptings.

Unfortunately, people who recklessly indulge in sin lose their sensitivity to the leading of the Holy Spirit. They could be compared to the unfortunate souls who have been struck down with leprosy—a disease that destroys a person's ability to feel pain. In fact, many lepers have become completely crippled simply because they lost sensitivity to bodily injury. This is a picture of the hardening that goes on inside a person who remains in unrepentant sin. His conscience becomes seared "as with a branding iron" (1 Timothy 4:2), burned so often that it can no longer feel the guilt of sin. As a tough callous forms over his heart, the spiritual system God constructed within him slowly loses its ability to detect the damage being done to it. No wonder Christian men in habitual sexual sin can sit in church week after week, singing songs of worship to a God they continually defy. "Hardened by the deceitfulness of sin," (Hebrews 3:13) their entire beings are consumed by the leprosy of evil which they can no longer even detect!

Repentance, of course, breaks up the fallow ground and softens the hardened heart. (Hebrews 9:14) Over time, the penitent sinner will regain his ability to hear "the still small voice" of God. With years of sinful indulgence behind him, he must then approach moral questions about sexuality with humility and the fear of making provision for the flesh.

Bearing that in mind, let us broach some of the subjects that commonly arise in the minds of believers. The following questions typify these issues surrounding sexuality:

Question 1: *Is it wrong for a married couple to engage in oral sex?*

This is a controversial question that can provoke strong sentiments. Many who believe oral sex to be sinful point to Romans 1: "For this reason God gave them over to degrading passions; for their women exchanged the natural function for that which is unnatural, and in the same way also the men abandoned the natural function of the woman and burned in their desire toward one another..." (Romans 1:26-27) They contend that the apostle is describing oral sex in this passage thereby proving it is wrong and "unnatural."

Personally, I'm not prepared to arrive at such a conclusive and comprehensive position. First of all, I believe Paul was condemning homosexuality in its entirety and that the specific activity engaged in was of secondary importance. If this were a legitimate line of reasoning, then sexual intercourse should be deemed wrong for the married couple because it is the practice of adulterers.

In regards to oral sex, there are two points I would make. First, God created sex to be a source of pleasure between a man and his wife. Dr. Ed Wheat makes this case in his excellent book, *Intended For Pleasure*:

> As a Christian physician, it is my privilege to communicate an important message to unhappy couples with wrong attitudes and faulty approaches to sex. The message, in brief, is this: You have God's permission to enjoy sex within your marriage. He invented sex; He thought it up to begin with. You can learn to enjoy it, and, husbands, you can develop a thrilling, happy marriage with "the wife of your youth." If your marriage has been a civil-war battlefield or a dreary wasteland, instead of a lovers' trysting place, all that can change. You see, God has a perfect plan for marriage, which we may step into at any time, and the mistakes of the past can be dealt with and left behind."[1]

Dr. Wheat is not here addressing any particular type of activity, but his statements express a very important truth, viz. sex was created so that a man and his wife may enjoy each other's bodies.

My second point is that what is right or wrong for one couple is not necessarily the same for another. To illustrate this, let's examine the love lives of three different couples.

Bill and Karen have been married for seven years. Bill was once heavily involved in pornography and various types of sexual sin. He enjoys both giving and receiving oral sex because both acts remind him of scenes in adult movies. Moreover, when he is on the receiving end he is much more prone to become emotionally detached and to fantasize about others than when engaged in normal sexual intercourse. For these two, oral sex is definitely wrong because Bill associates it with "dirty sex" and also because it encourages him to fantasize.

Phil and Ginger have a slightly different situation. Phil does not struggle with the same issues as Bill and desires to include oral sex in his foreplay with his wife. However, Ginger is not comfortable with either form of it. She feels that it is unnatural and does not want it to be a part of their lovemaking. Even though Phil doesn't associate it with anything sinful, it would be selfish and inconsiderate for him to impose his desires upon Ginger. He must simply drop the matter. The Apostle Paul's words would be appropriate for him: "Do nothing from selfishness or empty conceit, but with humility of mind let each of you regard one another as more important than himself; do not merely look out for your own personal interests, but also for the interests of others." (Philippians 2:3-4)

Our third couple to consider is Jim and Betty—who routinely engage in mutual oral sex. However, to them, it is merely a part of foreplay. Their motivation is that they love each other and are just trying to provide unselfish pleasure to the other. It is my belief that what is clearly wrong for the first two couples is not necessarily wrong for Jim and Betty.

These three situations show the importance of approaching a moral question with "a good conscience." In his discussion about the rightness and wrongness of eating food offered to idols, Paul laid down the following important principle regarding such issues: "I know and am convinced in the Lord Jesus that nothing is unclean in itself; but to him who thinks anything to be unclean, to him it is unclean." (Romans 14:14) Clearly, it is wrong for the first two couples to engage in oral sex. In the case of the third couple, I'm honestly not sure. However, I do believe this is a moral question that they should determine for themselves. Accordingly, God has given them each a conscience. If they are both in agreement that there is nothing "unclean" about this practice, then they must be given the latitude to make that decision for themselves.

Question 2: *My husband enjoys wearing women's undergarments as part of our lovemaking, even though he knows I don't like it. In response to my complaints, he maintains that his activity is acceptable since the marriage bed is undefiled. Is that true?*

Before discussing transvestitism, let us first set the record straight regarding the referenced verse. The wording used in this question is the King James Version of Hebrews 13:4—an unfortunate choice of words that has served as justification for all kinds of evil. Every other translation with which I am familiar gives a completely different sense concerning the meaning of the original Greek. The NIV is fairly typical of the rest: "Marriage should be honored by all, and the marriage bed kept pure, for God will judge the adulterer and all the sexually immoral." (Hebrews 13:4) One can easily see that the author's intent was not to sanction ungodly behavior but actually to promote purity in the marital bed.

In regards to transvestitism, it should be noted that the Bible directly forbids it: "A woman shall not wear man's clothing, nor shall a man put on a woman's clothing; for whoever does these things is an abomination to the LORD your God." (Deuteronomy 22:5) The fact of its prohibition could not possibly be more plainly expressed, and nothing exists in the New Testament that would annul this commandment.

However, even if transvestitism were not explicitly mentioned in Scripture, the very selfishness, coupled with the fact that the wife is uncomfortable with it, makes it morally wrong. Not only does it make this wife uncomfortable, but also it is selfish by its very nature. Transvestites (who are not typically homosexual) receive pleasure by wearing women's undergarments. This fetish is, by nature, completely self-absorbing and would therefore neither offer love nor bring pleasure to a man's wife.

Question 3: *My husband wants to purchase a video which teaches sexual techniques that is for sale in the newspaper. Is there anything wrong with a couple watching something like this in the privacy of their home?*

Do not be fooled by these slickly packaged videos for sale in the print media. Behind the protective facade of credibility and professionalism, they are actually nothing more than upscale pornography. Watching people having sex on a television set is very immoral—no matter how "clinical" the appearance. If the husband is sincerely interested in learning about how he and his wife can have a more fulfilling sexual relationship, I would encourage them to purchase a copy of *Intended For Pleasure*. It is a trustworthy book that provides forthright and helpful information without being prurient in content.

Allow me also to address the unconscionable notion of a Christian couple viewing pornography. Wives who assent to involvement in pornography usually do so to appease their husbands. The fallacy—all too often conveyed by the husband—is that, if he can watch it at home with his wife, their sex life will be enhanced and his sexual activity will be confined to the marriage. The problem with this faulty logic is that viewing erotica inflames a person's lust rather than satiating it. In fact, far from diminishing an existing problem, it actually accelerates it.

The effects of introducing pornography into the marriage bed are devastating, as I can personally attest. Early in our marriage, I convinced my wife Kathy to watch adult videos with me. Not only did it deepen my ravenous obsession with sex, but it also damaged her severely. In a letter to a wife considering this question, Kathy wrote about how pornography affected her and then asked the woman some direct questions:

> Had I only known what it would cost me, I never would have gotten involved in the first place. In my great determination to win my husband's love, at any cost, I was willing to sacrifice my self-respect, the morals I was raised with, and most importantly, my walk with God. For a long time, I was riddled with guilt and shame over the things I saw and did.
>
> But that wasn't all. It took years for those images to go away. For some time, I had to deal with unnatural desires I had never experienced before. Pornographic movies create the illusion that everybody is highly sexed and perverted. They warp a person's perspectives of other people. For a long time, I saw every woman as someone who wanted to seduce my husband, and every man as a pervert.

Having said all this, allow me to ask you some penetrating questions. Do you think it is right to be so given over to a man that you would consider degrading yourself with pornography just to keep the relationship together? What kind of a person will you have to become to keep him happy? Are you really willing to involve yourself with, and approve of, your husband's secret perversions? Do you realize, that becoming involved with pornography will only give your husband free license to openly lust over girls, in your presence? Are you sure you are willing to subject yourself to that?

Are you willing to involve yourself with something as evil and dark as pornography? Are you willing to walk away from God for the sake of appeasing your husband? Once you have hardened your heart against the Lord and filled your mind with perversion, what is going to stop you from taking the next step, and the one after that? These are questions you better carefully consider before taking that first step.[2]

Question 4: *I was previously addicted to pornography but I have been free from it now for over four months. Even though I have never been unfaithful with another person, my wife says she no longer loves me and wants a divorce. She claims she has grounds for divorce because of my involvement in pornography. Is that true?*

Before answering this question, I must state unequivocally that God hates divorce. (Malachi 2:16) Hates it! The Bible never uses this harsh term lightly regarding the Lord. When it says that He hates something, it means it is a great abomination to Him.

Unfortunately, Christians in our day and age often exalt their emotions above the Word of God. For a wife who "falls out of love" with her mate, the most viable option becomes divorce. If her pastor refuses to support her decision, she simply leaves his church for another. The fact that the divorce rate among Christians has actually climbed higher than that of unbelievers is a serious indictment upon the modern-day Church.

The Pharisees held this same flippant attitude toward marriage. If one of them became disenchanted with his wife for any reason, he would find a pretext to divorce her. Jesus told them, "Because of your hardness of heart, Moses permitted you to divorce your wives; but from the beginning it has not been this way. And I say to you, whoever divorces his wife, except for immorality, and marries another woman commits adultery." (Matthew 19:8-9) This teaching laid the groundwork for the only biblically plausible reason of divorce: unrepentant sexual sin. To say that a believer has grounds to end a marriage because of past wrongs when there is clear evidence of genuine repentance would go against the strong New Testament teaching regarding forgiveness.

In the aforementioned case, the man has repented and is making every effort to correct his past mistakes. Therefore, his wife's Christian duty is to forgive him for what is now in the past and reaffirm her commitment to him.

Nevertheless, it would still be beneficial to examine the bare question, "Is viewing pornography sufficient biblical grounds for divorce?" In the scripture cited above, Jesus makes allowance for divorce in the case of immorality (Gk. *porneia*). Although this term primarily describes fornication, commentators roundly broaden it to entail various kinds of sexual activity, i.e. incest, homosexuality, bestiality, etc.

Whether or not pornography use and masturbation would fall under this definition is debatable.

In situations where a husband is involved in unrepentant habitual sin, direct the wife to utilize the steps that Jesus laid down in Matthew 18 (as discussed in Chapter Five). If he rejects the process of church discipline and continually refuses to forsake his sin, then she should earnestly pray about a possible separation. If she sincerely seeks the Lord's will, He will surely make it known to her.

Question 5: *Is it sinful for a single young person to masturbate?*

Throughout most of Church history, Christian leaders considered any form of extra-marital sexuality to be sinful. Masturbation was rarely discussed openly. When it was addressed, it was usually cloaked in terms like "self-abuse," or biblical words such as uncleanness (Gk. *akatharsia*) or lasciviousness (Gk. *aselgeia*). Only during the past 30 years, as psychology has gained ever-increasing credibility within the Church, has it been suggested that masturbation is morally acceptable for a single person.

Is the modern Church's progressively open-minded, liberal position regarding sexuality simply a relaxation of stodgy, unnecessary rules of conduct from the Victorian age? Or could it be that today's moral laxity is further proof of the Church's relatively backslidden condition? While occasions do exist wherein believers remain needlessly old-fashioned regarding particular issues, for the most part it seems that Christendom has become enormously contaminated by the sexualized culture in which we live, following one step behind an increasing wave of decadence. In my opinion, the acceptance of masturbation by certain church leaders is a vivid illustration of this.

Seemingly, most of these relaxed standards have entered Christianity through the psychological community. Please understand that psychotherapy, by its very nature, is based more upon human empathy than biblical mandate. A counselor can sympathize so much with a person's struggles that he loses sight of God's expectation for holy living among His people. This approach can solidify itself in the counselor's heart if the power of God isn't actively at work in his counseling. Lacking any hope that the person can really overcome these overwhelming temptations, his only answer is one of acquiescence: The Lord understands that the habit of masturbation is too powerful for a young person to conquer. Therefore, it cannot be wrong.

Those with this mindset apparently overlook or minimize the truth of what Paul stated: "No temptation has overtaken you but such as is common to man; and God is faithful, who will not allow you to be tempted beyond what you are able, but with the temptation will provide the way of escape also, so that you will be able to endure it." (I Corinthians 10:13) A counselor who condones a habit simply because it seems too strong to overcome demonstrates a lack of understanding and experience of God's power to set the captive free.

Be that as it may, there are a number of reasons why I believe masturbation is wrong for the believer. First and foremost, God created sex as a means for a married couple to physically express their love to one another. It is a very special act, providing the closest possible intimacy two people can enjoy together. As has already been stated, marital sex affords the opportunity to a husband and wife to unselfishly provide mutual pleasure. And, of course, it is also the practical means for a couple to have children. Underlying all of this is the lifelong commitment and deep devotion that only a married couple can share. This is God's idea of sexuality.

Our modern, pleasure-driven culture holds an entirely different mindset toward sex. Those who purpose to fill their lives with the temporal gratifications of this world view sex as simply one room in the vast pleasure palace of life. Masturbation is considered a person's right—as are nearly all the various forms of pleasure available in our day and age. The difference between God's kingdom mentality and the pervasive world mindset can best be summarized by the words of Jesus: "If anyone wishes to come after Me, he must deny himself... For whoever wishes to save his life will lose it, but whoever loses his life for My sake, he is the one who will save it." (Luke 9:23-24) This is a perspective that worldly Christians refuse to embrace.

Whatever else may be said about masturbation, it is by its very nature a completely self-centered act. On a routine basis, the person isolates himself and enters into total self-indulgence. This kind of activity represents the very antithesis of the disciplined life Jesus expects from His followers and its selfishness is foreign to the Kingdom of God.

Furthermore, masturbation is driven by lust and fantasy. Sex is not meant to be a mechanical, physical activity comparable to relieving oneself in the bathroom. Inherently, it must involve another person—if not physically then mentally. To generate the sexual excitement necessary to bring oneself to orgasm requires that a person focus his thoughts upon someone else—a pornographic picture, the mental image of someone he has seen, or some sexual fantasy.

There are those who advocate fantasizing about some vague future mate as the solution to the masturbation dilemma. Of course, even if this notion was acceptable to God it is pure folly to think it is something that can actually be done. A young man has a hard enough time controlling his thoughts in everyday life. When he enters the highly sensuous mindset that materializes as he begins to touch himself sexually, it is next to impossible.

The best way to help a young single man is by imparting to him a godly mindset. If a son sees the primary focus of his parents' lives revolving around pleasure, entertainment and self-indulgence, then it is only natural that he will develop those same values in his own life. On the other hand, if he sees his parents living consecrated and unselfish lives, he is likely to follow this pattern. My experience has been that when a young man is taught to discipline himself, consecrate his life to God and live unselfishly, the temptation to masturbate will hold very little power over him. He may experience failures and setbacks but will consistently fight to maintain a pure heart before the Lord.

Rather than conceding victory to stubborn habits, the godly counselor must do his utmost to spur his counselees on toward holiness and teach them to trust God to provide the grace in times of temptation.

BOOK THREE

RUNNING A SUCCESSFUL SUPPORT GROUP

All Scripture is inspired by God and profitable for teaching, for reproof, for correction, for training in righteousness; so that the man of God may be adequate, equipped for every good work.

I solemnly charge *you* in the presence of God and of Christ Jesus, who is to judge the living and the dead, and by His appearing and His kingdom: preach the word; be ready in season *and* out of season; reprove, rebuke, exhort, with great patience and instruction.

For the time will come when they will not endure sound doctrine; but *wanting* to have their ears tickled, they will accumulate for themselves teachers in accordance to their own desires, and will turn away their ears from the truth and will turn aside to myths. But you, be sober in all things, endure hardship, do the work of an evangelist, fulfill your ministry. (II Timothy 3:16-4:5) twelve

THE BIBLICAL MODEL
FOR A SUPPORT GROUP

Small gatherings have always been an integral part of Christianity. Jesus Himself lived in a small group as He and His disciples traveled throughout the countryside together. Later, during the early days of the Church, believers quietly met together in various intimate settings. "And day by day continuing with one mind in the temple, and breaking bread from house to house, they were taking their meals together with gladness and sincerity of heart." (Acts 2:46) Throughout Church history, and especially during times of vehement persecution, small groups and home fellowships have played a crucial role in Christianity.

The intimacy a small group provides is an extremely valuable aspect of Christian life that few American believers have experienced. By contrast, the 25 staff members at Pure Life Ministries encounter this daily as they live and work together in community. Every weekday morning we come together for prayer and Bible study. It is not uncommon to see employees openly weeping and confessing sin before each other. As each person makes himself vulnerable in this way, it creates a greater degree of mutual love, trust, and support.

Additionally, the 53 men in our residential program also learn to live and work together in this manner.

This concept of a small group of men meeting together for the purpose of encouraging each other spiritually certainly has biblical and historical roots. In our present situation, where Christian men are continually bombarded with sexual imagery and temptation, support groups have emerged as the modern-day, streamlined method of providing aid to those who struggle.

However, as in any form of counseling, the effectiveness of support groups varies greatly. Some offer genuine help, while others actually do more harm than good. Major pitfalls can be avoided through a proper understanding of the dynamics involved in running a successful group.

THE GOAL

The initial driving force behind any new ministry is the founder's personal philosophy of ministry: a preconceived set of ideas that outline what he is trying to accomplish and the methods he will utilize to do it. The obvious goal in starting a support group for struggling men is to help them become liberated from habitual sin. The ultimate destination is FREEDOM through Jesus Christ.

The problem is that people have differing opinions on what it means to be "free." To some, freedom means no more than keeping habitual sin under a certain amount of control. Lacking an understanding of God's power to free a man from bondage, the best solution they can offer the man is life-long dependence upon "accountability." I discussed this issue in my book, *At The Altar Of Sexual Idolatry*:

I was invited to do an interview on one of the premier Christian radio talk shows about sexual addiction in the Church. During the days preceding the interview, I felt a growing conviction to convey to the radio audience the message that God changes people. I was determined to make the point that a man who is bound up in sexual sin has hope because of the transforming power of Jesus Christ.

However, the host of the program was equally determined to communicate his philosophy. His belief was that freedom from addiction rested upon the foundation of mutual accountability amongst others who are addicted. Each time I attempted to direct the conversation to the transforming power of Jesus, which can truly set all addicts free from their bondage, he would avert my efforts and emphasize the need for accountability. As we discussed in chapter four, accountability has its place in the restoration process, but it alone is not the solution to addiction. Its usefulness is short-lived for the person overcoming an addiction...

The common philosophy of dealing with addictions that the radio host, and countless others, advocate is that once a man is addicted to some vice, whether it is alcohol, drugs, gambling or sexual activity, he will *always* be addicted to it. This mentality is pervasive in various support groups where men open the meeting by going around the circle and saying, "Hi, my name is (Tim), I am a sexual addict." Though the man could have been walking in freedom for six years, he is still expected to identify himself with his past sin. Not only this, but he would also be expected to attend support group meetings for the rest of his life as his only means of escaping his addiction. He is a loser and must therefore always keep that in the forefront of his mind, lest he should go into delusion and return to his former lifestyle of sin.

Since most have little comprehension of or trust in God's power to change a person's life, their hope rests solely upon what they can do for each other; they are convinced that, to a degree, there is power within the "rooms" to maintain their sobriety. This "solution" has been termed "maintenance." It is based on the premise that an individual must learn to maintain his recovery from his sin. In other words, he must discover how to live his life in such a way that the sin is kept in abeyance. He is a victim of what is considered an invisible intruder that needs to be kept within certain boundaries. Instead of taking the wild beast out and mercilessly shooting it, it is respected and kept safely in a cage. The man attempts to control it, curb it, and stifle it, but he never becomes truly free of it. He is destined for a lifetime of a "white-knuckle" existence of being one step away from disaster, all the while professing a trust and belief in God.

Trying to "maintain" sin in this way keeps a person from being broken. Take Bob, for instance. He was a regular at the support group in his church for sexual addicts. He faithfully attended the meeting every Tuesday evening. He had been going for three years, admitting every time he would fall. He was always faithful to confess his failures, but it had become a routine of failure and confession. He never changed.

He later admitted that he had convinced himself that as long as he was going to the meetings and confessing his relapses with sin, God would be patient with him. His sin was not completely out of control as it had once been, but he had not gained any real victory over it. He had become comfortable with the arrangement.[1]

Not only do many group leaders have a weak concept of what constitutes liberty, their goals for those to whom they minister also fall short of God's desires. In an earlier chapter, I stated, "The number one objective of every believer should be to think and act biblically—to become more Christlike." With that in mind, allow me to present you with a hypothetical situation and then pose an important question.

Joe is a married Christian man who, for a number of years, has been addicted to illicit sex. He routinely visits strip clubs, massage parlors and street prostitutes. He enters the Pure Life Ministries' residential program and, upon graduation, never again returns to his old lifestyle. However, though free from outward immorality, he is still self-centered, angry and as full of pride, bitterness and lust as ever. Has Joe undergone the transformation that God desires for him? The obvious answer to that question is an emphatic "No."

Anyone who begins a Christian ministry—even if it is only a support group—is obligated to represent and extol Christ's values and expectations. Group leaders who proffer anemic solutions to deep-seated spiritual problems only exacerbate the situation. The gospel of Jesus Christ offers a degree of liberty that is neither feeble nor shallow; rather, it is deeply penetrating and all-encompassing. This level of change only requires brokenness and repentance—the biblical solution for those who struggle:

Each time one is broken by God, self loses that much control over one's life. The old nature, which loves the pleasures of sin, must be crushed. This can only come about through the mighty hand of God...

The person who attempts to "maintain" his sin cannot have true victory because his heart has not changed! Those who tell you that you must spend the rest of your life in support groups and in therapy do not understand the transforming power of a repentant heart. Many of them will never know about repentance because they will not allow themselves to be broken by God. Thus, their own hardened, unbroken hearts establish the basis for what they teach others. Out of that stony ground comes the kind of teachings that promote weak repentance.[2]

BIBLICAL ACCOUNTABILITY

Many of the support groups operating in today's churches have been founded by men who are themselves struggling with habitual sin. Believing accountability to be their primary solution, they start their own group which they attempt to lead, even though they themselves lack a personal testimony of freedom:

As I mentioned before, bringing secret sin into the open is vital. But biblical accountability was never meant to be a group of men sitting in a circle discussing their failures. Such a setting may be somewhat helpful to men who need to bring their sin out into the open with others, but there is no power in such a situation to bring about their needed deliverance.

A person can only lead another spiritually as far as he has gone himself. Jesus said, "...if a blind man guides a blind man, both will fall into a pit," (Matthew 15:14). It is helpful to a certain extent to open up with other people about one's struggles. But there is a biblical principle that is far more powerful in its ability to change lives. What men greatly need is to be discipled. "What do you mean? I've read all the books on sexual addiction. I've heard the best sermons on Christian radio. I just need a little bit of accountability!"

It might surprise the reader to find out that the word "accountability" is not mentioned once in the Bible. The concept is in Scripture, but not in the weak way in which it is currently used today. Instead, the biblical concept is that of being discipled. I am not referring to receiving more information about Christianity. Listening to good sermons and reading interesting books can be helpful, but what the immature Christian needs most is for a mature saint to take him under his wing, so to speak, and bring godly instruction into his life. (This is what we do in the Pure Life live-in program.) The spiritual growth that is necessary for the man who is in the grip of sin will not come about by simply talking with other struggling men, nor will it come by acquiring more head knowledge on the subject. It only comes through true discipleship—Christ-centered discipleship.

Jesus had those occasions when He spoke to the multitudes, but He spent enormous amounts of time building spiritual character into the small group of men under His care. A man may hear sermons, but unless he is held accountable to respond to those words, he probably will not benefit from what was said. The man is lost in a crowd of listeners. He can ignore, disregard, even disagree with what he is hearing, and is never required to face the truth of what is being stated.

However, when a godly man dedicates himself to discipling the struggling Christian brother, something powerful happens. Truth is imparted. Sin is dealt with head-on. The mentor expects change. Most importantly, the man experiences firsthand someone who is walking in the light and confronting him. This is the biblical pattern for accountability. It seems that in the busy lifestyle Americans live, pastors no longer have the time to mentor men as they once did. Sin is running rampant in the Church because Christians can now live out their lives without any true accountability for their actions.[3]

In the second chapter of this book, I discussed the spiritual qualifications of a person who can help others find freedom from habitual sin. I must reassert what I stated there: "A Christian leader can only take someone to the same depths he himself has gone." Until a man knows what it means to lay hold of God in a real and meaningful way, he is unable to encourage others to do the same. However, once he has established a godly pattern in his own life, he is ready to begin helping others do the same.

thirteen

BIRTHING THE MINISTRY

M y sincere hope at this point is that you clearly see spiritual preparation as a necessary prerequisite for involvement in the lives of others. The spiritual ramifications can be dangerous for those who foolishly plunge into people's problems without the proper spiritual resources or training.

Nearly as important as godliness and maturity is training. Anyone who seeks to help others—whether in one-on-one counseling or in a support group—must be trained in the proper application of Scripture. Paul said, "Be diligent to present yourself approved to God as a workman who does not need to be ashamed, accurately handling the word of truth." (II Timothy 2:15)

Unfortunately, most Christian support groups are led by those who feel that training is of no real consequence. The prevailing attitude of many can best be expressed in the words of one individual: "I'm not looking to become a counselor. I just want to provide a place where guys can get together and share their struggles." This lackadaisical approach is precisely why this man can offer no real help to his men.

The operation of a *successful* support group—one where men's lives are transformed—requires that the leader put forth the effort to prepare himself. You see, running a support group is really a form of counseling. The quality of the help that men are offered in your group largely depends upon the level of your godliness and preparation.

Another common attitude that diminishes a leader's perceived need for training is a brash confidence in his own knowledge of the Bible and ability to provide the answers men need. Few things are worse than a person with an inflated sense of his competency in helping others. By contrast, a good counselor or group leader functions with a certain sense of helplessness. He recognizes his inability to provide what his men need and humbly acknowledges his lack before God. He hungrily devours biblically-based teachings that will help him better understand people's problems. A persistent sense of inadequacy motivates him to press into God on behalf of those coming to him for help. The quiet confidence now growing within this maturing counselor is grounded not in his own capability to help others but on the fact that the Lord can and will help them.

Training not only helps you more effectively minister to others, but it also adds credibility to your work. As you begin promoting your ministry (talking to pastors and counselors, speaking in different groups and being interviewed on the radio), you need to present yourself as a capable leader. Proper training enables you to effectively articulate what you can offer to struggling men. As a result, the confidence you exude creates a level of trust in your audience. People can usually sense whether or not a person knows their subject.*

---

* This confidence is not built upon oneself but upon the truth and reliability of God's Word and upon the power and faithfulness of the Lord to meet people's needs.

A number of avenues exist for the aspiring group leader wishing to pursue training. The International Association of Biblical Counselors provides excellent training in biblical counseling.[1] Master's Divinity School actually offers a degree in counseling with an available tract which I helped develop entitled, "Counseling the Sexual Addict."[2] There are other reputable biblical counseling organizations that offer training as well.[3] All of these various course curricula are offered via correspondence. While course enrollment clearly offers more thorough training, there are also some outstanding books that have been written on the subject of biblical counseling.[4]

THE IMPORTANCE OF SPIRITUAL AUTHORITY

In order to successfully launch and operate a new ministry, you must have the support of your church. If you were seeking funding for a new business, you would begin by preparing a business prospectus for the bank. This is a systematic outline of what you intend to accomplish and how you will do it. If you are a member of a large church, I suggest you take the same approach with your pastor—even though you aren't looking for financial support.[5] Smaller churches tend to be less formal.

Whether or not you develop a prospectus, it is imperative that you receive the blessing of your pastor. Not only is submission to his authority a New Testament mandate, but there are a number of accompanying benefits. First and foremost, your submissiveness helps ensure that God's blessing rests upon your efforts. Peter said, "You younger men, likewise, be subject to your elders; and all of you, clothe yourselves with humility toward one another, for God is opposed to the proud, but gives grace to the humble. Humble yourselves, therefore, under the mighty hand of God, that He may exalt you at the proper time." (I Peter 5:5-6) Solomon put it more simply: "Humility goes before honor." (Proverbs 18:12)

If your pastor does not support your plans, DO NOT PROCEED UNTIL HE DOES. If and when he gets behind your efforts, his years of experience can be an invaluable resource and help as you face different problems or obstacles that arise. A good way to tap into your pastor's wisdom, without becoming a pest, is to write questions down as they arise and then share them with him in person or by e-mail. Secondly, your pastor's involvement can protect you in the event of false accusations. Lastly, having him behind you (or perhaps even promoting your work himself) gives you added credibility with other church leaders. This enables you to say to them, "If you have any questions or concerns, please feel free to contact my pastor." That statement alone silences fears and establishes credibility.

MINISTRY PREPARATION

The first practical decision you must consider is when to schedule your meeting. Some leaders prefer to have the group on Saturday morning. The greatest advantage to this is that men are fresh and more inclined to apply themselves to the information being presented. It is also less time constraining; the man still has all day to run errands and so on. Some groups even offer breakfast, but that tends to involve a lot of work and is better done occasionally. The downside to having a group on Saturday is that many men work on weekends. Summer weekend outings are another conflict.

The other option, of course, is to hold your meeting on a weeknight. This alleviates the Saturday problems and generally fosters a more solid commitment level. The biggest disadvantage is that men are often worn out from the work-day which can causes inattentiveness. One possible alternative, which has been adopted by some very well-attended ministries, is to offer a primary meeting during the week and a secondary one on Saturday mornings.

The location of the meeting is also important. The big question here is whether to meet in your church or elsewhere. For most, the advantages of hosting the group at the church outweigh the disadvantages. First, a church building usually provides suitable and professional meeting accommodations. Second, a church is typically much easier to find and access than, say, a private home. For instance, if you are appearing on a radio show, you merely need to mention the name of the church for the listener to mentally locate it.

However, there are some advantages to hosting the group elsewhere. First, meeting in a neutral location is less threatening for other pastors who are sending their men. Pastors are notoriously reluctant to send members of their flock to another church. Another inherent advantage to meeting at a private site is increased anonymity for the participants. One negative aspect to meeting at your home is that, depending on its size, it can quickly become fairly crowded.

The actual location within a metropolitan area is one more thing that should be seriously considered. I know of one man who held meetings in his downtown office, forcing his men to drive through a seedy area to get there. Easy access to a freeway is another significant factor.

The next step is to establish a phone number that can be posted and advertised. For a number of reasons, I would strongly suggest installing a second phone line in your home. First, it can have its own answering machine with a message identifying your ministry: "Hello. You have reached the Victorious Men hotline. We hold support group meetings every Tuesday evening at 7:00 p.m. at Victory Church, on Victory Blvd. If you would like me to return your call, please leave your name and phone number after the beep…" This method provides men with pertinent information about your group and also allows them to contact you personally. Secondly, for those with a wife and children, it is not a good idea to give out your home number to men who are struggling with sexual sin. Although it is rarely a problem, you never know who might call that number. Besides that, it can be a little unnerving for a tentative caller to hear a female voice on the other end of the line. Lastly, a second phone line makes it convenient to screen calls when you are with your family. If finances are an issue, you may have to trust God's provision for the extra line.

Once you have established a phone number and mailing address (usually a post office box), you are ready to produce a ministry brochure and perhaps even business cards and stationery. This can be a very effective promotional tool for informing others about your new work. As a rule of thumb, a professional-looking brochure adds credibility. The overall expense of designing and printing 1,000 brochures can range anywhere from $500 to $1,500. A less expensive option is to design it yourself on your own computer and make copies. Whichever route you choose, your brochure should contain all the vital information: when and where you meet, telephone number, mailing address, and, if possible, the curriculum you will be using. More importantly, you must share your heartfelt goals for the men who attend your meetings.

You can often place brochures at churches, men's ministry groups and sometimes at Christian bookstores. Of course, you should also hand them out to everyone you contact regarding your ministry.

PROMOTION

Once you have "your ducks in a row," the next step is to begin actively promoting your ministry. Spreading the word about a newly established support group can be a full time job!

A good starting point is to contact the hosts of any talk shows on the local Christian radio station. Send a brochure and accompanying letter explaining what you are doing and your desire to help those in their audiences who struggle with sexual temptation. If you haven't heard from anyone within a couple of weeks, call the hosts at the stations. They are probably very busy and so you can assume they never saw your letter. Briefly introduce yourself and invite the host to lunch at a nice restaurant near the station. If you have the opportunity to meet together, humbly share your burden with him. At this point in the process, there's a good chance he may have you as a guest on his show.

In the event that you are unable to get on a local talk show, be sure to ask the station receptionist whether they air a community calendar. If so, they can probably mention your group periodically.

Another idea is to visit the pastors of churches in your area. You can help alleviate a pastor's concerns by assuring him that you are not interested in stealing his sheep. Rather, your desire is to do everything possible to encourage his men toward more active involvement in their own church. If he seems cooperative, you could ask about the possibility of placing ministry brochures in the church foyer. He might even allow you to share the vision of your ministry with an adult Sunday school class.

Another significant group to approach with your idea is area men's ministry leaders. Your support group can be an

invaluable resource to them as they encounter men struggling with sexual sin. You may be invited to share in an existing group or at a local men's breakfast. It would also be wise
to network with any local Christian drug and alcohol support groups. Finally, contact all Christian counselors practicing in your city. Perhaps they might consider your group as
an important supplement to their counseling.

As you meet and talk with community leaders, word will
gradually spread to those who need the help you offer. In a
short time, you will have a group of men meeting regularly
each week.

MANAGING A GROWING GROUP

An effective leader understands the principle of delega-
tion. Moses learned this lesson the hard way, exhausting himself physically and emotionally while trying to do everything
himself. Finally, Jethro, his father-in-law, convinced him to
appoint seventy elders who would help bear the responsibility of leadership. You probably won't need the assistance of
seventy leaders, but a couple of dedicated helpers could sure
be a blessing!

As your group grows and becomes unwieldy, you can
divide the men into smaller groups. To manage this you need
to seek out trustworthy helpers. You should insist upon certain attributes in a potential subgroup leader. First and foremost, is the man maturing as a Christian? Is he personally
walking in victory over sin? (An occasional slip in masturbation for a single man should not be a disqualification.) Has
he shown a serious commitment to the ministry? Has he
been faithful in his attendance? Does he appear competent
in his dealings with others? Is he well-liked and respected by
the other men? Do they seem to trust him? Is he humble

and teachable? Do you sense that his willingness to help comes from a real burden for the men or out of some selfish motivation? Is he an active listener? If he is lagging in a few of these areas, perhaps you can work with him. Potential is key so allow room for the possibility of growth. However, a complete deficiency in any of these areas is probably a good indication he would not work out. For instance, how could you rely on a man who excels in every category mentioned above but is inconsistent in his attendance? Or, what sort of example would he be to others if he does not seem interested in maintaining a personal devotional life? Moreover, what if he simply lacks the ability to interact with people? As you can see, a lapse in one area can quickly disqualify a man for leadership.

Even if an individual demonstrates great promise, it is important not to rush him into leadership too quickly, lest you ruin him. (I Timothy 3:6) I have seen it happen many times: A guy is doing well until he is given a position of authority. Then it goes straight to his head and, before you know it, you have an unruly monster on your hands. It is best to take it as slowly as possible. Just to give you an example, staff members at Pure Life Ministries typically undergo at least twelve months of extremely intense discipleship in a communal setting before being placed in a leadership position. Granted, leading a small group is not the same as being a counselor in a facility, but the same principles apply.

If you feel that a particular man has leadership potential, spend as much time with him as possible. Teach him everything you know. This same principle is applied by Paul in Timothy's life as he instructs his young apprentice: "And the things which you have heard from me in the presence of many witnesses, these entrust to faithful men, who will be able to teach others also." (II Timothy 2:2)

As your ministry develops a reputation in local Christian circles, new men will continue to show up at the meetings. Some will attend regularly while others will be more sporadic.

In order to help these men, it is vitally important that you maintain regular, open communication with them. A telephone call once a week to faithful attendees can serve as a real source of encouragement to them. Occasionally, your call may be divinely arranged to arrive during a time of real temptation. What a blessing to be there for a man in his moment of weakness!

It is also important to call new attendees at least once. Since most men are hesitant to come to a meeting that centers around sexual sin in the first place, a follow-up phone call is a good way to welcome the newcomer and express your sincere concern about him. Consider delegating the responsibility of some of these calls to an assistant.

A support group that is properly run can be a wellspring of help and encouragement for struggling men. Nevertheless, they often need more help than what is afforded by the support group setting. Additional counseling, outside of the group setting, can sometimes be beneficial.

As mentioned earlier, you must invest time in those you identify as potential helpers. This requires that you become more involved in his life through deeper discipleship and even individual counseling. Barring any negative response to your personal involvement, the goal of this is to enable him to build into the lives of other men.

Occasionally, you will feel compelled to work more closely with other individuals in the group who seem to be struggling. Some guys really want freedom from their habitual sin and yet still routinely struggle. A weekly support group meeting is not sufficient; they need personal attention. A man who appears sincere in his desire to overcome his problems is often a valid candidate for more individualized counseling.

It is worth mentioning that, in the course of your work, you will also discover women in need of attention. Primarily I am referring to wives of men in sexual sin, but you may also be contacted by a woman struggling with sexual sin herself.

Never counsel women by yourself.* If your wife wishes to join in your work, she can make herself available to help others. Of course, it goes without saying that, if she is going to become involved in people's lives, the same spiritual and educational requirements hold true for her as well.** If she chooses not to become involved, you should direct the inquiring woman to her pastor's wife.

When Pure Life Ministries was just a support group in Sacramento in the late eighties, our men's group was regularly attended by 25-35 men and our wives' group usually consisted of a dozen women. Kathy, my wife, began the group for wives and ministered to them for several months. She eventually handed her responsibilities over to another woman whom she herself had ministered to and discipled.

These are some of the practical issues you will face when starting a support group for men in habitual sexual sin. While it is certainly important to understand and implement these different strategies when starting a group, just as essential is knowing how to actually run a meeting.

---

* I also urge you not to allow struggling women to join your support group. There are secular 12-step groups that offer co-ed meetings, but this is extremely hazardous. A person's intimate details should not be shared in a mixed group.
** Another possibility is that she will counsel women for a period and later replace herself with another qualified lady.

fourteen

RUNNING THE GROUP

H aving successfully promoted and established your ministry, now the real work of managing it begins. Your supreme task is to build a support group meeting that will keep men interested enough to stay involved while at the same time offering them genuine help. Again, this will require a much more systematic and diligent approach than the lackadaisical attitude held by many who typically run such groups.

A properly-run support group revolves around foundational principles of true discipleship. As I mentioned in an earlier chapter, discipleship involves the four-fold use of Scripture outlined in II Timothy 3:16 – teaching, reproof, correction and training. Let me briefly restate the purpose of each of these terms:

- Teaching: General instruction in victorious Christian living;
- Reproof: Withstanding a man who is drifting away from God;
- Correction: Adjusting faulty, unbiblical thinking;
- Training: Personal instruction about a man's specific situation.

Whenever possible, you should implement these tools in your meetings. The most effective way I have found is to divide your meeting into two parts: a time of teaching and a time of accountability.

A TIME OF TEACHING

In the Sacramento group meetings I led many years ago, I always gave a sermonette during the first half hour on a topic related to sexual sin. Although I was very "green" at the time, I poured my heart into these messages. In fact, some of the subjects I covered in those early days formed the basis for much of my book, *At the Altar of Sexual Idolatry*. Among the topics I addressed were temptation, the process of sin, lust, repentance, the world's influences, etc.

If you intend to teach your men, you must diligently prepare your message with the aim of articulating truth in such a manner that retains their interest. Keep in mind that it is a sacrifice for most of the men to come to your meeting. Once they sense that your heart is not in it, many will simply quit attending. Also be aware of the principle that you are there to help *them*. One author aptly described the selfish thinking some small group leaders develop:

> Leaders protest, "I worked on this lesson for seven hours. It's not fair to me when you don't do the assignment. All my work goes to waste!" Translation: "I worked hard to create something you ought to listen to. Because I created it, you should want to hear it. After all, you exist to provide an audience for my teaching and leading skills. If you don't do your part, how am I ever going to have a ministry?"[1]

Always remember that you are there to help and bless the lives of others. If those men sense that the underlying motive of your ministry is to somehow gratify yourself, they will quickly lose interest. On the other hand, if they feel that you truly care about them and are doing your best to help them, to a large extent they will overlook a lack of ability.

Ideally, you should begin preparing your talks well in advance of actually delivering them. Conveying information gleaned from the writings of others can be helpful, but nothing is as effective as sharing some spiritual truth that God has made personally real to you. A personal Bible study of related topics helps bring them alive to you and the men as you later teach them.

The Word of God is the most effective tool for preparing a meaningful talk, but studying the writings of other men can also be beneficial. Be careful, however, that what you read and convey to others is solidly corroborated by Scripture. Do not waste your time reading books that are built upon faddish notions and weird ideas (i.e. speaking to your inner child, sitting your "self" in an empty chair and forgiving yourself, etc.). The safer, more productive route is to stick with truths having a firm Scriptural foundation.

If you feel inadequate to teach, don't despair! There are alternatives. Let me offer you four possibilities that various small group leaders (who have been loosely affiliated with PLM) have utilized.

First, numerous groups have used my book, *At The Altar Of Sexual Idolatry*, as a source for teaching material. Typically, they read a section and then spend time discussing the principles outlined. Of course, group reading can be a tricky matter. If you allow everyone to take a turn reading, the inevitable scenario occurs: at least one man present is not a good reader. The minutes drag on excruciatingly for the others as he labors over every word. However, if you do all the reading yourself, the lack of participation might result in boredom for some. Fortunately, this pitfall can be avoided if you read a paragraph at a time with intermittent periods of open discussion.

We also know of other groups that give their men homework during the week in anticipation of the next meeting. The workbook that accompanies *At The Altar Of Sexual Idolatry* contains questions relating to each chapter which the group leader can assign as homework.* Each chapter also includes a set of questions specifically designed to stimulate group discussion. The homework approach greatly benefits the men by reinforcing in the meeting what they have spent time studying during the week. Thus, rather than attempting to cover everything on meeting night, the gist of the teaching is communicated before the man arrives.

There are also studies available that were created for the sole purpose of compelling an individual to consult Scripture regarding a particular topic. Three that come to mind are: *Experiencing God*, by Henry Blackaby; *Lord, How Can I Be Righteous*, by Kay Arthur; and *Self-Confrontation*, by John Broger. I recommend any of these. Additionally, I should mention that every participant in a Pure Life counseling program is required to go through *The Walk of Repentance*, a Bible study I developed. Each of these courses is appropriate for use as a men's group study as well as being an excellent tool for an individual's daily Bible devotions.

Lastly, group leaders may choose to employ audio and/ or video tapes with pertinent teachings. Of course, Pure Life Ministries offers both, but you need not limit yourself to

---

* In Chapter Seven I discussed the role homework plays in the counseling process. One of the benefits of it is to discover a man's level of sincerity.

teachings that directly address sexual immorality. There are other (more general) subjects that have been taught or preached that are very relevant to men bound up in habitual sexual sin.

Some group leaders integrate multiple methods of instruction. One week the men listen to a teaching tape. The next week they read portions of *At The Altar Of Sexual Idolatry*. The following week the leader himself teaches on a subject, and so on. Another alternative is to use one of the above methods for several weeks and then switch to another for a period of time. By mixing a variety of teaching modes, you decrease the risk of monotony and losing the men's interest.

GROUP RULES

Before discussing the accountability portion of the meeting, it is important to point out the fact that every small group must operate under a set of rules. These guidelines can be expressed verbally or in writing. I suggest outlining them on a sheet that is given to every newcomer.

The first "rule" I recommend is that each participant agree to maintain strict confidentiality about what is shared in the meeting. In a support group for those struggling with sexual sin, men need the assurance that others will not gossip about anything confessed. (This commitment to secrecy is not sufficient cause to keep you from reporting a serious crime that comes to your attention, i.e. child molestation).

Another essential principle is the need for openness and honesty. Making oneself vulnerable to others in such an intimate setting is extremely valuable for spiritual growth, especially if the person is struggling with secret sin. Encourage each participant to be frank about his struggles (within certain guidelines). If one person refuses to make himself vulnerable, others may find it more difficult to do so as well. (These expectations should not immediately be placed on newcomers.)

Another principle requiring strict adherence is sensitivity concerning the use of language and explicit details. A discussion among a group of men about sexual sin can cross boundaries in a moment's notice. This usually occurs for one of two reasons: Either a man is oblivious to how his words are affecting others or he is purposely trying to achieve some form of selfish gratification. If one group member begins to tell a story which might cause others to stumble, firmly but gently interrupt him at once, urging him to refrain from his current course of conversation.

LEADING THE GROUP

Crucial to the success of any support group is that the conversation stays on course. As the leader, you are responsible for maintaining control of the discussion. In fact, if you don't control it, someone else will, and I can assure you that his interests will be selfish. The following are a few examples of the different personality types that could steal "the show" from you:

"Depressed Derrick" relishes group settings because he loves to get everybody involved in his pity party. The highlight of his life is manipulating people into feeling sorry for him. If left unchecked to verbalize his negative and faithless feelings, he not only draws attention to himself (and away from the needs of others), but he also drains the life out of the meeting. Clearly, there is a place for encouraging the downcast. However, Derrick has no interest in receiving encouragement so that he might re-enter the battle with renewed enthusiasm; he simply covets the attention and pity of everyone present.

"Controlling Curt" is another one to watch for. Although gifted with natural leadership abilities, he has not submitted himself to the Lord. He desires to lead others but not to be led himself. Of course, in the Kingdom of God, a man can only lead others spiritually to the degree that he himself is submitted to and controlled by the Holy Spirit. Curt, being a know-it-all, is not interested in being taught. He is an opportunist—viewing the group meeting as a chance to teach and lead others rather than a place to get help. Solomon aptly describes this self-made leader: "A fool does not delight in understanding, but only in revealing his own mind." (Proverbs 18:2)

"Talkative Ted's" incessant chatter will drive you "right up the wall!" If you do not keep him reined in, he will dominate the meeting with his endless, pointless babbling. One experienced small group leader described this person to a tee: "If not moderated properly, what often begins as a trickle of friendly patter can turn into a virtual flood of words. The Talker is rarely shy, and usually very uncomfortable with long periods of silence. Typically, what's behind this need to fill in the pauses is the fear of intimacy or personal disclosure."[2]

On the flip side, "Quiet Ken," who prefers to remain silent, would be perfectly happy if Ted did all the talking! Ken is not disruptive and his struggle is honest. He is socially awkward and often freezes up in the midst of a group setting. He must be treated with patience, love, and a great deal of sensitivity.

While each of these personalities can be challenging, if handled properly, they will not disrupt or ruin the meeting. In reality, when dealing with such people you face a bigger challenge from within yourself. The following are examples of feelings that can paralyze your leadership:

- Experiencing false guilt for not allowing Derrick to "dump on" the group;
- Being intimidated by "Controlling Curt;"
- Being too timid to shut down "Talkative Ted;"
- Feeling unqualified to lead others.

Keep in mind that these feelings are common, and, as such, you may experience them in your ministry. There are steps you can take that will greatly aid your efforts at maintaining control over the group along with minimizing the debilitating effects these feelings have on your leadership ability.

First, establish from the outset the way your meeting will function. This is of utmost importance since most Christian men are accustomed to support groups being a verbal free-for-all. Generally speaking, the easiest way to win a battle with strong personalities is to strongly establish your own leadership up front. Lay down the ground rules in the beginning, rather than making them up during the meeting. This informs newcomers of how the group operates and also serves as a constant reminder to the others that you are the leader. Here is an example of what you could say:

I want to remind everyone of the ground rules of our support group meeting. I will be interviewing each of you and everyone will have an opportunity to share. I ask that you only speak when it is your turn because we are limited in time and I want to make sure that everyone has an equal opportunity to share. It is extremely important that this doesn't turn into a "gab session." Therefore, during the first part of our accountability time, I must insist that you refrain from making comments. After we have gone around the circle once, there will be a time for everyone to share their opinions or questions.

THE INTERVIEW

Instead of allowing personalities to dictate the flow of your meeting, you can control the course of conversation through the interview process. Here's how it works. Let's say there are seven men in your group. If you want the accountability portion of the meeting to last an hour, you can spend about six minutes talking with each man and still leave 18 minutes left at the end for a free sharing time. By regulating the amount of time you spend with each individual, you can assure "Quiet Ken" of having an opportunity to share while reining in "Talkative Ted." As an added benefit, this prevents "Controlling Curt" from taking over the meeting. You might even use a kitchen timer that rings at the end of the allotted time. This shifts the focus off you as the terminator of that man's session.

After opening with prayer, turn to the man next to you and ask him how he did during the past week. His answer determines the course of your interview. If he fell into sin, the following are some questions you might ask: "How did it happen? What were the events leading up to your fall? How did you have the time, opportunity and/or money to accomplish it? Does your wife know what happened? Is there anything she could have done to prevent it from happening? What were your devotional times like last week? What can you learn from this failure? What could you do differently next time? Why didn't you call me when you were tempted?"

If, on the other hand, he did well that week, the natural inclination is to assume there is nothing to talk about and quickly move on to the next guy. Actually, this situation affords you the opportunity to become more personally acquainted with him. The following are questions you could ask that may help him to open up to you: "Do you have any victories to report? How are things going with you and your wife? How are things going on the job? What would you say is the source of your greatest temptation?" Depending on his responsiveness, this conversation can take on a life of its own. (Biblical counseling training provides valuable interview techniques applicable to all situations.) When your time with him concludes, he should feel as though something meaningful has been accomplished.

Having finished with him, move on to the next man and so on until you have gone all the way around the group, then allow some time for people to openly converse. One man might have something useful to share with another. Limit this time to reduce the risk of someone like Curt exerting leadership. After you conclude the meeting with prayer, be open to the possibility of some of the guys staying behind for informal fellowship.

EFFECTIVE INTERVIEWING

A number of important elements are involved in conducting a successful interview. As a general rule, they can be summarized in two categories: how you listen and how you speak.

As a group leader, learning to be an active listener is crucial. Solomon said, "A wise man will hear and increase in learning..." (Proverbs 1:5) James said, "...let everyone be quick to hear, slow to speak and slow to anger." (James 1:19) I have seen many leaders who are just the opposite—slow to hear, quick to speak and quick to anger! In essence, being quick to hear means you concern yourself more with other people's needs than on your own desire to talk. Your interest level in that man is evidenced by the way you listen to him. A perceived lack of care on your part may produce superficial dialogue.

One way you can be an active listener is by following up his statements with probing questions that encourage deeper reflection. For example: "How has your three weeks of victory affected your relationship with your wife?" Another example: "You said that you felt empty and miserable after you fell into sin. Can you describe those feelings in greater detail?" These questions provoke the interviewee to share from his heart.

Another method for use in conversation is paraphrasing what you have heard the individual say. This, too, promotes further depth of response. For example: "I think what I hear you saying is that sometimes you struggle with wanting to serve God; that there are those periods when you just don't seem to care. Did I express that correctly?" Another example: "If I understand what you are saying properly, your wife doesn't seem to care about your frustrations at work. She seems unconcerned about how they affect you. Is that what you meant?" Summing up what someone says provokes him to share more about what he is feeling, while assuring him that you are really listening.

Perhaps even more important than the way you listen to people is the way you speak to them. Solomon's wisdom says much about the effect words can have on another. Consider the contrast between the speech of the fool and that of the wise man: "There is one who speaks rashly like the thrusts of a sword, but the tongue of the wise brings healing." (Proverbs 12:18) "A gentle answer turns away wrath, but a harsh word stirs up anger. The tongue of the wise makes knowledge acceptable, but the mouth of fools spouts folly." (Proverbs 15:1-2) "The heart of the wise teaches his mouth, and adds persuasiveness to his lips." (Proverbs 16:23) "A fool does not delight in understanding, but only in revealing his own mind." (Proverbs 18:2) "A fool's lips bring strife, and his mouth calls for blows." (Proverbs 18:6) I think you get the picture. The manner in which you speak to men determines their level of trust in you.

Moreover, the spirit you are in will also dictate the course and atmosphere of the meeting. If you show up at the last minute, hurried and harried, buzzing with adrenaline, you will very likely be carnal and impatient with the men during the meeting. On the other hand, arriving early and spending time preparing your heart in prayer will more likely enable you to handle the meeting in a calm and loving spirit.

Remember, words can convey strong messages so be careful what you say. The following are some pithy rules to live by:

- Do not criticize or make fun of a person in front of others.
- Do not give pat answers.
- Do not be sarcastic, defensive or condescending.
- Do not give an answer before hearing the whole story. (Proverbs 18:13)
- Do not be afraid to admit you presently don't have the answer to a problem.
- Whenever possible, do not correct a person in front of others.

Prayer in the Group

It is critical that you maintain a spiritual atmosphere within the meeting. A group of men can very easily "get in the flesh." However, if you open your meeting in prayer and maintain a sober atmosphere, it should have a subduing effect on any who tend to be unruly. The quality of your prayer life plays a significant role in this kind of situation. If you have a superficial devotional life, your opening prayer may come across as shallow, apathetic, and ineffective (no matter how much energy you try to imbue into it). Conversely, if you are interceding for your men every morning, it should be evident as you pray in the meeting. Don't be afraid to pray with intensity and earnestness. Heartfelt prayer touches both God and men and establishes the atmosphere for the remainder of the evening.

Encourage the men to pray for each other at home, as well. In accountability meetings held at the PLM live-in facility, men are taught to be very attentive to those who are sharing. They are instructed to jot down notes about what other men are struggling with so that they can pray specifically for them during the week. This practice also encourages active participation in the meeting, even when they are not talking. Rather than being bored by lack of involvement in the conversation, they tend to be more interested in what is being expressed. The knowledge that others are going to be praying for them inspires them to do the same. Intercessory prayer goes a long way toward fostering mutual support and deepening friendships. As time goes on, the inevitable result is a more cohesive and caring group.

The end of the meeting should also be closed in prayer. This is a good opportunity to allow a guy who is doing well to pray.

HANDLING DISRUPTIONS

Problems do occasionally arise, so you must be equipped to handle them when they do. In Chapter Five, I mention the procedure Jesus established for handling sin. Let us re-examine this biblical blueprint with regards to handling problems within the group setting:

> And if your brother sins, go and reprove him in private; if he listens to you, you have won your brother. But if he does not listen to you, take one or two more with you, so that by the mouth of two or three witnesses every fact may be confirmed. And if he refuses to listen to them, tell it to the church; and if he refuses to listen even to the church, let him be to you as a Gentile and a tax-gatherer. (Matthew 18:15-17)

This passage of Scripture supplies the proper method for dealing with disruptions in the group. For instance, let's say Curt keeps speaking out of turn and "button-holing" people with his advice after the meeting. The first thing you should do is talk to him privately, humbly explaining to him why his behavior is unacceptable. Be sympathetic, realizing that his actions are simply a reflection of who he is as a person.

If he fails to change his behavior, then, in the company of one of your assistants, speak to him personally again. You also have the option of involving your pastor into this process. At the very least, inform your pastor of the situation in case it gets out of hand.

If he still refuses to alter his actions, then you must tell him he is no longer welcome in your meetings. Explain to him that you would like to help him with his struggles but he doesn't seem desirous of your assistance. Tell him that if, in the future, he is willing to abide by your rules, the door is open for him to return. Hopefully, he may eventually see his need for your help and may humble himself to receive it.

These principles will not only help you run a successful support group meeting but will also provide a structured format to allow the Lord to effectively work in men's lives.

As I have already expressed, countless lives and families have been devastated by immorality in the Body of Christ. There is a great need for spiritually mature saints to reach out to and help those in the grips of habitual sexual sin.

You have but one life to give away for the cause of Christ. My hope and prayer is that this book has encouraged you to become "a friend of sinners" by bearing them, interceding for them, discipling them and loving them. If you will do this with all your heart, God will use your efforts to produce much fruit for His Kingdom. May He richly bless your work in the lives of those in need!

BIBLIOGRAPHY

INTRODUCTION

1. Steve Gallagher, *At the Altar of Sexual Idolatry*, Pure Life Ministries, 2000.
2. Scott Covington and Curt Swindoll, *Pornography: No Longer a Dirty Little Secret*, www.NetAccountability.com.
3. *ibid.*
4. MSNBC/Stanford/Duquesne Study, Washington Times 1/26/00.
5. Christianity Today, *Leadership Journal*, December 2001.

CHAPTER ONE

1. Steve Gallagher, *Break Free From The Lusts Of This World*, Pure Life Ministries, 2001.
2. Archibald Thomas Robertson, *Word Pictures in the New Testament*, e-Sword Software (www.e-sword.net).
3. Dr. John Gill, *John Gill's Exposition of the Entire Bible*, e-Sword Software.
4. Adam Clarke, *Adam Clarke's Commentary on the Bible* e-Sword Software.
5. Albert Barnes, *Albert Barnes' Notes on the Bible*, e-Sword Software.
6. *The Expositor's Bible*, AGES Software (www.agessoftware.com).

7. Matthew Henry, *The Matthew Henry Commentary*, AGES Software.

Chapter Two

1. Adapted from *We Are Becoming What We Love* from the book *God Tells The Man Who Cares* by A.W. Tozer, copy right 1992. Used by permission of Christian Publications, Camp Hill, PA. For a complete listing of A.W. Tozer products, log onto www.christianpublications.com or call 800.233.4443.
2. Steve Gallagher, *ibid.*

Chapter Three

1. Steve Gallagher, *Irresistible to God*, Pure Life Ministries, 2003.
2. Geoffrey W. Bromley, *Theological Dictionary of the New Testament*, William B. Eerdman's Publishing Co., 1985, p.645.
3. Steve Gallagher, *Break Free from the Lusts of This World*.

Chapter Four

1. Dr. Jay Adams, *Christian Counselor's Commentary on I & II Corinthians*, Presbyterian and Reformed Publishing, p.34.

Chapter Five

1. William Hines, *Leaving Yesterday Behind*, Christian Focus Publication, 2002.
2. Steve Gallagher, *ibid.*

Chapter Six

1. C.H. Spurgeon, *A Popular Exposition to the Gospel According to Matthew*, AGES Software.
2. Dr. Jay E. Adams, *The Christian Counselor's Manual*,

Presbyterian and Reformed Press, 1973.

Chapter Seven
1. Adapted from a talk given by Amy Knicely-Baker, Ph.D.
2. Written for *Unchained Magazine* by Pastor Brad Bigney, Pure Life Ministries, Vol.1, Issue 3, 2002, p.24-25.

Chapter Eight
1. Kathy Gallagher, *When His Secret Sin Breaks Your Heart*, Pure Life Ministries, 2003.
2. Steve Gallagher, *At the Altar of Sexual Idolatry*.
3. Kathy Gallagher, *ibid.*
4. *Ibid.*
5. *Ibid.*
6. *Ibid.*

Chapter Nine
1. Dr. James Dobson, Focus on the Family website; *Ask Dr. Dobson*. The study he cites is by Michael J. Bailey and Richard C. Pillard, "A Genetic Study of Male Sexual Orientation", Archives of General Psychiatry 48 (December 1991): 1089-96.
2. *Ibid.*
3. Kathy Gallagher, *ibid.*
4. Steve Gallagher, *At the Altar of Sexual Idolatry*, *ibid.*

Chapter Eleven
1. Dr. Ed and Gaye Wheat, *Intended For Pleasure*, Fleming H. Revelle Co., 1977, p.14.
2. Kathy Gallagher, *ibid.*

Chapter Twelve
1. Steve Gallagher, *ibid.*

2. *Ibid.*
3. *Ibid.*

CHAPTER THIRTEEN

1. The International Association of Biblical Counselors, www.iabc.net or call (303)469-4222.
2. Master's Divinity School, www.mdivs.edu or call (800)933-1445.
3. National Association of Nouthetic Counselors, www.nanc.org or call (317)337-9000;
Biblical Counseling Foundation, www.bcfministries.org or call (760)773-2667;
Christian Counseling and Education Foundation, www.ccef.org or call (215)884-7676.
4. Dr. Jay E. Adams, *Competent to Counsel.*
5. Joseph Covello, *Your First Business Plan*, Hazelgren Publishers; Grossman, Raha & Kravilt, *How to Raise Capital: Preparing and Presenting the Business Plan.*

CHAPTER FOURTEEN

1. Bill Donahue, *The Willow Creek Guide to Leading Life-Changing Small Groups*, Zondervan Publishing House, Grand Rapids, MI, 1996, p.13.
2. *Ibid*, p.133.

RECOMMENDED READING
FOR BIBLICAL COUNSELING

Beyond Seduction, Dave Hunt

Christian Psychology's War on God's Word, Jim Owens

Competent to Counsel, Dr. Jay E. Adams, Zondervan
Publishing Co., 1986

How Christian is Christian Counseling?, Dr. Gary Almy,
Crossway Publishers, 1999

Introduction to Biblical Counseling, Dr. John MacArthur, Word
Publishing, 1994

The Biblical View of Self-Esteem, Self-Love and Self-Image,
Dr. Jay E. Adams

The Christian Counselor's Manual, Dr. Jay E. Adams,

The Handbook of Church Discipline, Dr. Jay E. Adams

The Sufficiency of Christ, Dr. John MacArthur, Word
Publishing, 1991

Why Christians Can't Trust Psychology, Dr. Ed Bulkley,
Harvest House, 1994

INDEX OF SCRIPTURES

INDEX OF SUBJECTS

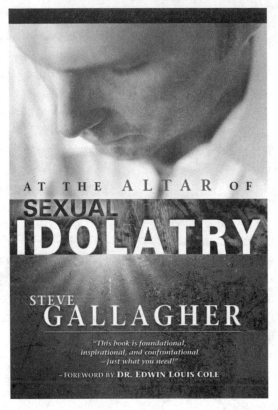

WHERE TO TURN WHEN SEXUAL SIN DEVASTATES A MARRAIGE.

What can be more devastating for a wife than to discover her husband has a secret obsession with pornography and other women? Yet, this is what countless Christian wives face every day. Kathy Gallagher has been there; she understands the pain of rejection, the feelings of hopelessness and the questions that plague a hurting wife. In this collection of letters, Kathy imparts heart-felt encouragement by providing the practical, biblical answers that helped her find healing in the midst of her most trying storm. The 30-day journal offers wives a place to prayerfully reflect and meditate upon Kathy's letters.

The Walk of Repentance

The Walk of Repentance is a 24-week Bible study for any Christian that desires to be more deeply consecrated to God. Each week of this easy-to-use curriculum has a theme, addressing the everyday challenges believers face one step at a time. Its simplicity is its strength, using only the Word of God—and occasional stories of saints of old—as its content. Experience the times of spiritual refreshing that follow repentance; go deeper in God as you allow His Word to take root in your heart.

Videos

Breaking Free From Habitual Sin

People try all kinds of methods to break sinful habits, but God has only given one answer to habitual sin: Repentance. Find the freedom you seek; allow the Lord to tear down your old way of thinking and loose the chains that bind you.

Overcoming Insecurity

Insecurities... how many of us have felt their paralyzing effects; yet, how few of us recognize them as the blight of pride? Allow the Lord to dismantle those crippling defense mechanisms that keep you from the abundant Christian life.

When the Temple is Defiled

Christian men in sexual sin often need a wake-up call, a message that pins them to the floor in repentance. This sermon, filmed at Zion Bible Institute during a day of prayer and fasting, describes what happens to those who desecrate their inner being with pornography and sexual sin. God's presence was very strong and used this message to spark great repentance.

Audio CD

Breaking Free From the Power of Lust— *Our Most Popular Series!*

The insidious beast of lust can entrap a person to the point of hopeless despair, but the Lord has given answers that work! The biblical revelations imparted in this series will break the power of lust in the believer's heart. (Four CD's)

Also Available on 4 Audio Cassettes

PURE LIFE MINISTRIES

Pure Life Ministries helps Christian men achieve lasting freedom from sexual sin. The Apostle Paul said, "Walk in the Spirit and you will not fulfill the lust of the flesh." Since 1986, Pure Life Ministries (PLM) has been discipling men into the holiness and purity of heart that come from a Spirit-controlled life. At the root, illicit sexual behavior is sin and must be treated with spiritual remedies. Our counseling programs and teaching materials are rooted in the biblical principles that, when applied to the believer's daily life, will lead him out of bondage and into freedom in Christ.

BIBLICAL TEACHING MATERIALS

Pure Life offers a full line of books, audiotapes and videotapes specifically designed to give men the tools they need to live in sexual purity.

RESIDENTIAL CARE

The most intense and involved counseling the staff offers comes through the **Live-in Program** (6-12 months), conducted on the PLM campus in Kentucky. The godly and sober atmosphere at Pure Life Ministries provokes the hunger for God and deep repentance that destroys the hold of sin in men's lives.

HELP AT HOME

The Overcomers At Home Program (OCAH) is available for those who cannot come to Kentucky for the live-in program. This twelve-week counseling program features weekly counseling sessions and many of the same teachings offered in the Live-in Program.

CARE FOR WIVES

Pure Life Ministries also offers help to wives of men in sexual sin. Our wives' counselors have suffered through the trials and storms of such a discovery and can offer a devastated wife a sympathetic ear and the biblical solutions that worked in their lives.

PURE LIFE MINISTRIES
14 School Street
Dry Ridge, KY 41035
(859) 824-4444—Office
(888) 293-8714—Order Line
inquire@purelifeministries.org
www.purelifeministries.org